SUPER BOWL

Of Men, Myths and Moments

SUPER BOWL

Marty Ralbovsky

Foreword by Howard Cosell

An Associated Features Book

HAWTHORN BOOKS, INC.
Publishers
New York

SUPER BOWL

PHOTO CREDITS

For Kevin

May he grow up in search of the truth

ACKNOWLEDGMENTS

The author thanks the following players and former players for their cooperation and straightforwardness: Fred Williamson, formerly of the Kansas City Chiefs, now a regular on the "Julia" television show and the only actor to resemble a football player in the closing minutes of M*A*S*H; Curtis McClinton, director of the Black Economic Union in Kansas City and a former Chief; Jim Tyrer, of the Chiefs, and Bob Skoronski, Gale Gillingham and Donny Anderson, of the Green Bay Packers.

Also, Don Chandler, the former Packer now in real estate in Tulsa, and Phil Bengtson, the former Green Bay coach now on the staff of the San Diego Chargers. The author also acknowledges the following non-players for their assistance: Bill Matney, White House correspondent for the National Broadcasting Company; Chuck Lane, the Packers' public relations director; Bill Hamilton, the Chiefs' public relations director; Lou Prato, of Station WWJ-TV in Detroit, and Larry Ruppert, who helps run half-time shows for professional football out of an office aptly located in the Disneyland Hotel in Anaheim, Calif.

The author expresses his gratitude to the following contemporaries for allowing their volumes to be used as reference material: Dave Anderson, *Countdown to Super Bowl;* Todd Hunt, *Packer Dynasty;* George Sullivan, *My Life in the Pocket: The Story of Earl Morrall;* Lou Sahadi, *The Long Pass,* and Jerry Izenberg, *Championship.*

He is also grateful to *The New York Times* for the unlimited use of its nonpareil reference library; to Phil Berger for the use of his personal collection of football data, and to Ira Berkow and Murray Olderman, of Newspaper Enterprise Association, both of whom contributed considerably more than a couple of yellowed columns.

The author also wishes to thank Zander Hollander, of Associated Features, who not only conceived the book but also guided its development with a sensitive hand, and a young lady named Susan Ralbovsky, a virtuoso on typewriter keyboards and the complement supreme.

M. R.
New York City

CONTENTS

FOREWORD

Only five Super Bowl Games have been played. The event lacks tradition. Yet it ranks with a heavyweight championship fight and the World Series as one of the three super events in American sport.

One reason is the popularity of professional football itself. It is a game for its time. The principal characteristics of the contemporary society are swiftness and contact — some say violence. These are the essence of professional football.

The anticipation that precedes a Super Bowl is greater than that which precedes any other event with the sole exception of a heavyweight championship fight. This is because there is only one game to be played and that's it. No second chance. No tomorrow. Unlike the World Series.

The manner in which the Super Bowl came about also lends a continuing uniqueness to its impact. The struggle of the American Football League for parity, the legend of invincibility that attached to the National Football League, and then the beginning of the showdowns — could those other fellows really play in the Big League? — all this has lent an aura of special excitement to the contest.

Author Marty Ralbovsky captures this in the book SUPER BOWL. And much more. He fulfills the role of the true journalist by not only reporting the play-by-play when it counts, but by delving into the personalities of the key figures on and off the field. Perhaps the book's greatest value is in this approach, its emphasis on human beings. All events come and go. Namath and the Jets won one year. Namath was booed to death the next. But Namath survives while the game is history.

The revelations of a Fred Williamson, why he popped off before the first Super Bowl, the reactions of his teammates, the behavior of his coach . . . these are the things that take you inside the event, give it the absolute flavor of why a Super Bowl game is special, why it carries with it an extraordinary anticipation.

Unlike baseball, but much like boxing, one man is pitted against another physically. The drama is in a Buchanan against a Thurston, the redemption of Bubba Smith, the incessant pride of Vince Lombardi in his league, the insecurities and doubts of a Dave Herman.

This is what the Super Bowl is all about. It's what this book is all about, insightfully written, not tied to the clichés of the sportswriters of the past.

HOWARD COSELL

xi

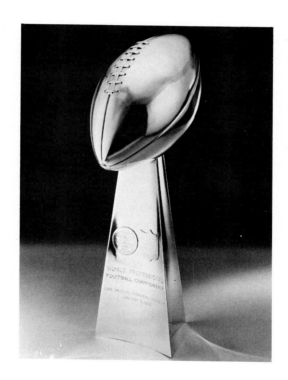

INTRODUCTION

Like moon walkers, miniskirts, and My Lai, the Super Bowl is a product of the 1960's, a phenomenon made possible by the elements and the mentalities of the decade. It did not evolve naturally, as fetuses develop into healthy, screaming newborns; it was manufactured on an assembly line and placed onto the conveyor belt called merchandising, which has no peer in the art of penetrating the minds and emotions of America, arousing fervor in both. That the Super Bowl has become the most popular single sports event in the United States after only five playings tells as much about the state of the country as it does about the state of the game.

Dr. Joyce Brothers, the psychologist with an affinity for sports, has said that the success of an organized sport depends upon the cultural priorities of the country in which it is played. America in the 1960's was preoccupied with violence: Sociopolitical assassinations, civil uprisings, and battlefield deaths in far corners of Asia had become as commonplace as nightly reports on closing prices on the stock market. To seek the illusion of violence had become an acceptable, if not desirable, means of temporary escape from the very real violence of a throbbing world that threatened to shimmy itself off its own axis.

The appetites for violent fantasies were spoon-fed by the very terminology of pro football, with its bombs and its blitzes, its bumps-and-runs, and its power sweeps, not to mention the nicknames of some of its teams — the Chargers and the Raiders to name two. The illusion of mock warfare on Sunday afternoons on color-television screens added a measure of zest to otherwise regimented households, and the savoring of it superseded the more conventional weekend rides along rustic country roads in autumn and, yes, even the lovemaking to anxious spouses, alone in the house with dirty laundry and dirty dishes during the uneventful week.

Emotionally spent and physically limp after watching as many as three pro football games on a single Sunday, the television fan craved only for his supper and his slumber after the ordeal. The fan who had spent the afternoon in the stadium came home and more often than not craved only a hangover cure. Ignored wives and children even went as far as feigning interest in the electronic pygmies, figuring that a shared FatherFan was better than none at all; and surely, during commercials, perhaps, he would recognize their presence with a nod of the head, at least. What they wound up doing, though, was trading expletives with him after fifty-five-yard runs and enraging him if they dared distract him from the instant replays of them. The effect pro football had on American family life in the 1960's is fodder for future psychologists: It made the living room a good place in which to be together while being apart.

The Super Bowl itself was conceived after the marriage of two less-than-compatible pro leagues. For nearly a half century the National Football League had monopolized pro football in America, but in 1960 competition emerged in the form of a new league, the American Football League. In 1966, after six years of jockeying for position for money from fans, recognition from the media, and signed contracts from top college players, the adversaries sat down and hammered out an agreement that would, by 1970, consolidate all of professional football under a single roof and eliminate the overhead caused by their rivalry. It was called a merger; it was more of a mutual accommodation. The National League, holding the pat hand of identity, made outrageous financial demands on the insurgent group, which just as outrageously agreed to them in the name of equality. One of the few concessions granted the newer league was that its best team would be allowed to play in a game against the best team of the National League for the theoretical world championship of professional football.

Alvin Ray (Pete) Rozelle, a former public-relations man for the Los Angeles Rams who in 1960 was the compromise choice of NFL owners as their commissioner and later the overwhelming choice of both leagues as the head of their combined household, suggested that the titular game be called "The NFL-AFL World Championship Game." Had the name been sanctioned, the pretentiousness would have surpassed that of baseball, which steadfastly called its pro playoff the "World Series" while refusing to recognize professional leagues in Japan, South America, Mexico, and other assorted countries. A true "World Series," surely, would be international in scope, not limited to American teams from, say, Cincinnati, Ohio, and Baltimore, Maryland.

At least baseball *was* played in other countries on planet Earth, and "World Series," although an inaccurate and inappropriate term, could be dismissed as a mere reflection of American braggadocio; but only Canada, out of the rest of the world, played a game that resembled pro football: Surely one half a hemisphere could not implicate the rest of a planet in its own creation. Other names for the game were thrown into the family hopper as if to head off the pomposity. Some team owners suggested calling the game "The Big One," and "The Final Game," indications of their enthusiasm if not their emptying wells of creativity. The Super Bowl finally got its name by accident, however, as absurdly as a man naming his child's puppy after a favorite breakfast cereal.

Lamar Hunt, owner of the Kansas City Chiefs and one of the most influential men in pro football during the 1960's, blurted out the name "Super Bowl" while sitting in at a joint meeting of AFL and NFL owners, and the strained minds embraced it triumphantly. Hunt, disclaiming any secret courses in merchandising, said the credit should not go to him but rather to his young daughter.

One night Hunt returned home with a toy for her. It was a Silly Putty ball, which the girl favored immediately. While chasing it around the house a few nights later, she told her father that the ball was capable of doing amazing things and that she had made up a special name for it.

"It's my 'super ball,'" she said.

SUPER BOWL I

DESIRE

Participants — Kansas City Chiefs, champions of the American Football League, and Green Bay Packers, champions of the National Football League.

Date — January 15, 1967.

Site — Memorial Coliseum, Los Angeles, California.

Time — 1:05 P.M., EST.

Attendance — 63,036.

Radio and Television — National Broadcasting Company (TV and Radio), Columbia Broadcasting System (TV and Radio).

Regular-Season Records — Kansas City, 11-2-1; Green Bay, 12-2.

Playoff Records — Kansas City defeated Buffalo Bills, 31-7, for AFL title; Green Bay defeated Dallas Cowboys, 34-27, for NFL title.

Players' Shares — $15,000 to each member of winning team; $7,500 to each member of losing team.

Gate Receipts — Estimated $730,000.

Radio-TV Receipts — $2,000,000.

Officials — Referee, Norm Schachter, NFL; Umpire, George Young, AFL; Linesman, Bernie Ulman, NFL; Back Judge, Jack Reader, AFL; Field Judge, Mike Liteski, NFL; Line Judge, Al Sabata, AFL.

Coaches — Hank Stram, Kansas City; Vince Lombardi, Green Bay.

KANSAS CITY, Jan. 4 (UPI) — The Kansas City Chiefs, champions of the American Football League, left today for Long Beach, Calif., where they will prepare for the Super Bowl football game against the Green Bay Packers on Sunday, Jan. 15, in Los Angeles. Coach Hank Stram said his team would practice immediately after arriving at the training site, and that the workout would not be open to the press or to the public.

"On the airplane, somewhere between Kansas City and Los Angeles, I realized this team was scared to death," said Fred Williamson, left corner back for the Kansas City Chiefs. "I looked around me and all I saw were zombies. These guys were scared of playing the Green Bay Packers. They were scared of playing in the first Super Bowl, scared of the unknown. Sheeit. Some of these guys would rather have had the plane go down.

"So I said to myself right then and there, 'Hammer, there's only one guy around here who can snap this club out of it — you.' I had to show these guys that we weren't going out to the coast to lick the Packers' boots. So after we landed at the Los Angeles airport and boarded a bus for Long Beach I devised my plan. First I had to put pressure on myself and show these clowns that I could take it and that I wasn't afraid of the big ol' Green Bay Packers like they were. Then I had to put the pressure on them and hope that they would react the same way. So many guys had copped out to themselves already that I knew we were going to get our asses

2

whipped unless something drastic happened to wake them up.

"That first day in Long Beach, a bunch of reporters came around and one guy asked me what I thought of Jim Taylor. I said to him, 'Jim Taylor, sheeit. He ain't so hot. Jim Nance runs harder than he does.' Another guy asked me about Boyd Dowler. I said, 'Boyd Dowler isn't any better than Art Graham.' Their faces were blank, and I could see they didn't know who Art Graham was. So I told them, 'Art Graham plays for the Boston Patriots — once in a while.' Then some guy asked me about Carroll Dale. 'Carroll Dale, sheeit,' I said. 'He's about as good as Glenn Bass of Buffalo, and you know what happened to Glenn Bass. He lost his job in the middle of the season.' Well, those sportswriters couldn't get it all down fast enough, and I kept saying to myself, 'Hammer, you're beautiful, man. They ain't never seen a cat like you before.'

"Later that day I went out and rented myself a limousine, one of those big black jobbies all shined up and looking like the devil's own. Then I went out and bought some suits and ties, nothing but the sharpest stuff. It was time to play it to the hilt. The next time those reporters and television and radio guys were going to see me, I'd be stepping out of my limo, lookin' prettier'n Lena Horne, big-timing it over to them like I was the King of England or something. Once they put their eyeballs back in, I'd tell them, 'Green Bay Packers, sheeit. We're gonna whip their asses.' It was no boolshit, either. That's the way I was feeling. If the Super Bowl was Fred Williamson against Jim Taylor, one on one, I knew I'd whip his ass. If it was Fred Williamson against Bart Starr, ol' Bart, he ain't got a prayer. But those clowns I was playing with, man, I had to get them feeling the same way. They see me peacocking around, maybe they'll pick it up, maybe they'll start saying, 'Green Bay Packers. Sheeit.' Whether they like me or not, personally, who cares?

"That night, the papers started coming out and all those big black headlines were saying that ol' Fred The Hammer Williamson was going to take the Packers apart single-handedly if he had to. I was strolling through the lobby of the motel and some of the guys were standing around, and when they saw me coming they looked straight at me and I could see the angriness in their eyeballs. Then they looked the other way and I said to myself, 'Oh, oh. They ain't mad at the Packers, Hammer. They're mad at *you.*' I bought myself some papers and went up to my room, and when I started reading what the other guys were saying I really flipped out, man. They were licking boots. Johnny Robinson, he tells a reporter he just finished watching movies of the Packers and that it didn't look too encouraging. Robinson said, 'The Packers are just a great, great team. I've never seen anything like it.' And Dave Hill, who's going to be playing opposite Willie Davis. Somebody asked him about Davis and he said, 'If Davis is as good

Fred Williamson would bring his celebrated "Hammer" into the Super Bowl. In this sequence during the regular season, with Buffalo's Glenn Bass the victim, Williamson stalks his prey with his right arm cocked; drops his Hammer, stunning the receiver; and then completes the wipeout.

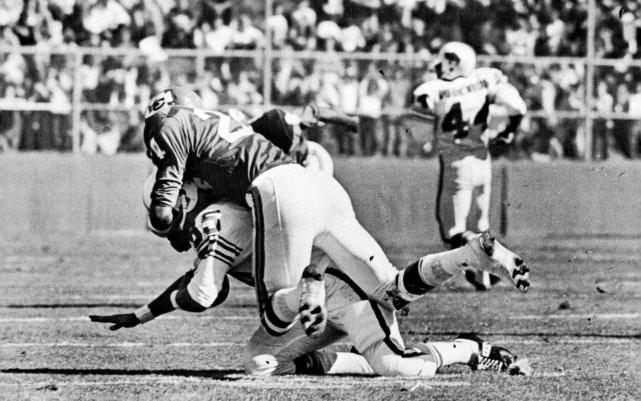

as he is supposed to be, and I do a decent job, I'll feel pretty good. I'll know then that I can play against the best there is.' What boolshit.

"So I kept talking, hour after hour — the Packers, sheeit, Taylor, sheeit, Lombardi, sheeit. We're going to whip their asses, all of them, and if Boyd Dowler and Carroll Dale or any of those other guys have the nerve to catch a pass in my territory they're going to pay the price, man. I'm going to lay a few hammers on 'em and they're going to go back into the huddle with their heads ringing like they're hearing chimes and their eyes full of stars and dots and their legs twanging like rubber bands. Then they're going to tell ol' Bart Starr, 'Bart, baby, throw to the other side, man, throw to the other side.' Two hammers on Dowler, one on Dale should be enough.

("The Hammer" was what Williamson called the clothesline-like blow he administered to the helmeted head of anyone who dared tread in his territory. He described "The Hammer" to *The New York Times* as "a karate blow having great velocity and delivered perpendicular to the earth's latitude." He described it to others as "a lethal muthah.")

"The third day on the coast, the Packers hadn't arrived yet, so the writers and TV guys were following me around night and day, calling my room, hanging around the motel restaurant, leaving messages for me to call them. When I went through my messages, there was one from Hank Stram, the coach. It said he would like to see me. I went up to his room and he said, 'Fred, a lot of the guys are unhappy about some of the things you're saying. They feel that you're giving the Packers impetus.' I said, 'Boolshit, coach. I'm trying to give *them* impetus, not the Packers. Besides, the Packers aren't even here yet. They're still in Green Bay.' So he said, 'Didn't we warn the entire team back in Kansas City to watch what was said to writers, to avoid making any statements that would fire the Packers up? Didn't we say that, Fred, and weren't you there listening?' I said, 'Yes, coach. But what you're telling me is boolshit, man. You're just as bad as the rest of them. You tell the papers that we're not going to deviate from what we've been doing for the last six months, that we're not going to add anything to the offense or the defense. They are your exact words, coach, I read them — *We're not going to dee-veee-ate, we're not going to add anything.* That's boolshit. Why don't you tell them you've added so many new plays and formations the guys are having a helluva time learning them all? Why don't you tell it straight, man? I've never seen so many X's and O's and dotted I's as I've seen in the last few days. You should be telling them that we're going to come out there in the Los Angeles Coliseum with so many new plays and formations that we're going to have the Packers taking notes.' Stram didn't say anything after that, he knew it was hopeless.

"But this showed me something about Stram. All year long he'd been telling me, 'Freddie, you're just the guy we needed around here. You're a leader. We've got a young club and all we've lacked in the past is a leader.' So all season long I'm talking to the guys, firing them up, and they're buying it all, man. I know I'm putting confidence into this team, and Stram, he goes around saying he's behind me all the way and I'm just what the doctor ordered. Then we win the league championship and we make it to the first Super Bowl game and he tells me, 'Fred Williamson, shut up.' Boolshit."

> *GREEN BAY, Jan. 8 (AP) — The Green Bay Packers will leave today for their Super Bowl training camp at the Santa Barbara campus of the University of California. The team will fly to Santa Barbara, where it will practice until Jan. 13. After two off days following the National Football League title victory over the Dallas Cowboys, the Packers spent the week reviewing films and studying scouting reports on the Kansas City Chiefs.*

"Just before we left Green Bay to fly to Santa Barbara, Vince called us all together," said Bob Skoronski, offensive tackle for the Green Bay Packers. "He said to us, 'A week from today, nobody is going to leave that stadium until the job is done. I'll keep you there all day, all night, all week, if necessary, until you win. There is no way the Green Bay Packers are going to lose this football game.'

"I had never felt such a sense of urgency on Vince's part before. It was obvious to all of us as we started the flight to the Santa Barbara airport that never before had we played in a game that Vince Lombardi wanted to win more. During the week in Green Bay, Vince was a man possessed. He was a nervous wreck, very tense and irritable, snapping at anyone who made even the most microscopic mistake. He was really hooked on this thing about carrying the banner for the NFL. He would read to us letters and telegrams from NFL people — I remember two in particular, from George Halas and Wellington Mara, because he was really touched by them — and they all said the same thing, that they were happy the Green Bay Packers were going to represent them in the Super Bowl and that we should go nail the coonskin to the wall.

"When the bus that took us from the airport to the motel stopped in front of the place, I remember Vince saying 'Oh, no' to nobody in particular. He got off the bus and looked at the mountains that surrounded our motel and his face dropped. He stopped Phil Bengtson, the defensive coach, as he was getting off the bus and he said to him, 'Phil, these mountains, what is this? This place is like a resort. We want something barren. I don't want these guys looking at mountains all day. Their minds will start wandering. . . . Phil, I've got it. Let's run the plays away from the mountains, toward

7

the ocean.' Bengtson said, 'Okay, the offense will work facing the water, the defense facing the mountains.' Vince said, 'Good. I like that.'

"The first few practice sessions were reminiscent of training camp back in Wisconsin. Vince was stressing conditioning and, truthfully, a lot of us couldn't understand why at that stage of the year. One of the guys — I don't remember exactly who — said to Vince in the motel lobby, 'What're you trying to do, coach, get us in shape this week?' Vince answered him with a glare. Some of us were thinking that Vince might have been concerned about miscalculating the Chiefs. What if they were a lot better than he thought they were going to be? The answer, of course, is to resort to brute strength and power and grind them down. But we had to be in shape to do it. We all figured that he was making sure that we were — just in case.

"The daily schedule was as planned-out as an army recruit's. Vince had every minute mapped out for us. There was no time at all to yourself. Vince would take care of any extra time by telling us things like, 'I want all players on the bus parked near the main lobby at nine-thirty in the morning. Do you hear me? Nine-thirty in the morning.' So we'd all get there at nine-fifteen or so and we'd grab a seat and be ready to go. But Vince would tell the bus driver not to leave until ten o'clock. It was his way of using up forty-five minutes of our time.

"He gave us the clichés, too, as soon as we got there. He would say, 'You players from that 1960 team, the team that made it to the championship game and lost to Philadelphia, you guys made a commitment to yourselves that you would never let yourselves get that far again — and lose. Do you still have that commitment?' And Fuzzy Thurston or Max McGee or myself would always say, 'Yes, coach, it's still there.' And he would say things like, 'How would you like to have a lifesaving merit badge and not be able to swim?' And nobody would know what he was talking about. The key to the whole thing was not what Vince said, but how he said it. He had a way of romancing these things until they started gnawing at your insides.

"The first few days in California were the most tense of the season. The schedule, the conditioning, the seclusion and the discipline were starting to get to us. The guys were edgy, some were mean as hell. But Vince was still pushing, still working on us. He stopped several of us one morning after breakfast and said, 'There is one more thing I want to stress upon you people. I don't care how many friends you have on that team. I don't care how many guys you played with in college, or how many guys you played with in high school. I don't care. Understand? Sunday, there will be no brother-in-lawing.' "

9

Coach Lombardi's workouts left no time for viewing the scenery.

LAS VEGAS, Jan. 8 (UPI) — The Green Bay Packers were made eight-point favorites over the Kansas City Chiefs today in an early betting line for the Super Bowl game in Los Angeles on Jan. 15.

"Fred Williamson's motives were suspect, as far as I was concerned," said Jim Tyrer, offensive tackle for the Kansas City Chiefs. "The guy was always looking for attention, not for the Chiefs, not for the defensive unit, but for himself, Fred Williamson. He was throwing a lot of half-truths around and I think he put a lot of unnecessary pressure on himself and Willie Mitchell in the defensive secondary.

"Williamson was the only guy on the team flapping off at the mouth. The rest of us were working. Myself, the feeling inside of me bordered on ecstasy. I was mesmerized by the magnitude of the game. Hell, this was the biggest game in the history of football and here I was, a part of it. The anxiety was incredible, but I had control of it. I kept telling myself, 'Everybody's a rookie going into this game.' I knew the Packers were a sound football team, but I wasn't exactly awed by them. I didn't hate them, either, not like I hated the Oakland Raiders, if 'hate' is the right word to use. Nothing personal, it's just that Oakland represented something I disliked immensely. Tom Keating and Harry Schuh are good friends of mine, but when they go out on the field in those black and silver uniforms, they're no longer my friends.

"Almost all of the players, not counting Williamson, of course, were intense as hell. The life-style at the motel contributed to it. The whole scene was like training camp again. The coaches were making bed checks, and every minute of the day was planned out for us. Personally, I liked it that way. I was a lot older than most of the guys, and I had played in a couple of AFL pressure games before, and I knew the value of seclusion. It's a lot easier for an older guy to break away from his family for a week or two than it is for a young, single guy to break away from his night life. My off-season job required a lot of traveling, anyway, so my family was used to it. Heck, I was kinda happy to get away from them during this period so I could concentrate on football. Somebody asked me, 'How's the family?' I told him, 'I don't know.' I didn't worry about them at all. I had great confidence in my wife. If anything came up, I knew she would call."

LOS ANGELES, Jan. 9 (UPI) — Football Commissioner Pete Rozelle expressed confidence today that the Super Bowl game would fill Memorial Coliseum to its capacity of 93,000. Answering reports that ticket sales had been slow, he said:

"After all, we've just been going through the holi-

days, and fans have been preoccupied by the college
bowl games. I think sales will show a sharp increase
this week and the game should be a sellout."
Tickets are priced at $12, $10, and $6.

"I really didn't feel part of the whole scene," said Don Chandler, place-kicker for the Packers. "A kicker is in a funny position. I'd practice my punting before the rest of the team practiced, and my place-kicking after it practiced. The rest of the time I'd hang around with the defensive unit, listening to what was said and pretending to be part of it. But I really wasn't. I was the odd man. To make it worse, this Super Bowl game would be the last one in the poorest season I'd ever had in football.

"I hadn't been kicking well all year and when I'd go out to the field early in the morning to punt, all the bad kicks I made during the season would float through my head. I'd kick fifty-five punts a morning. In the afternoon, I'd kick fifty field goals from different ranges. The same thing would happen — all the bad ones would haunt me. There was nobody to talk to about it, so I had to live with it myself. When a kicker is going bad, he's all alone. There's nobody around to slap you on the rump and tell you, 'That's all right, man, get 'em next time.' No, sir. It's like you're part of the team, but not really a part of it. Know what I mean?

"I was thinking that week, too, about retiring from football. Hell, I knew I could keep kicking for another ten years if I wanted to, once I got my confidence back. But I wasn't too sure I wanted to keep living like this. I had some real estate and some property holdings back home in Tulsa, and I had a wife, two little girls and a boy, and maybe the time had come to stop running around the country kicking footballs and living in strange hotels, eating strange food, and meeting all kinds of strange people. 'One more year,' I was telling myself one morning while punting, 'one more, maybe, and that's it. Twelve years are enough.' "

"Even though I was a rookie, I wasn't awed by the Super Bowl," said Gale Gillingham, offensive guard for the Packers. "I wasn't awed by anything that year because I realized very early that the Old Man didn't want any guys around who were starry-eyed. I realized that in training camp, and I said to myself, 'Okay, even if I am scared, I'll never show it.'

"Funny thing, but I didn't enjoy being a Packer. The guys were all right, and they had this attitude about rookies that wasn't bad at all. They'd accept you right away if they thought you could do them some good. If you couldn't, well, that was a different story. I was playing behind Fuzzy Thurston, and I knew I'd be getting his job and so did everybody else, it was only a matter of time. I knew I wouldn't start the Super Bowl game,

11

Veteran Don Chandler and rookie Donny Anderson had their own practice.

but I knew I'd be playing in it sometime. Maybe I didn't feel a genuine part of the Packers yet, I don't know. But it wasn't fun, it wasn't enjoyable, not like college ball. It might have been because of the things that happened in training camp — I didn't particularly like some of the rituals they had for rookies. The singing business, for example, took more out of me than any of their two-a-day drills.

"I just hated singing songs every night for eight weeks. Here we were at this St. Norbert's College, up in the Wisconsin sticks, and nuns are around and the kitchen help and the janitors and the whole team, including the Old Man. I'd have to get up on a chair in front of all of them and say, 'My name is Gale Gillingham, and I'm from the University of Minnesota, and tonight I'm going to sing such-and-such.' Then I'd sing some song, usually one I had been practicing, but sometimes I'd sing whatever came into my head. If I wasn't loud enough, they'd all scream and yell and make me start all over. If I blew a line or two, same thing. I hated it more than anything I ever had to do in my entire life. I'd as soon have faced a firing squad. The thought of singing would start bugging me in the afternoon practice. After dinner the veterans used to go out and have a beer or two and we rookies used to go back to our rooms in the dorm and study our sheet music, or listen to records and memorize the words. I didn't think that was right.

"But the Old Man used to tell people that he could tell more about a guy's character by the way he sang than he could by the way he played football. I never could understand that. I had this thought running through my mind that maybe, just maybe, the Old Man and the rest of the Green Bay Packers were just a bunch of sadists."

> *KANSAS CITY, Jan. 10 (UPI) — Burglars who broke into the Kansas City Chiefs' headquarters yesterday apparently were not football fans.*
>
> *They made off with an undisclosed amount of cash, but left behind 2,000 tickets to the Super Bowl game. A club spokesman said that the thieves apparently had gained entry by forcing open a furnace-room door and then peeled off the door to the walk-in safe. He did not disclose the amount of cash taken.*

"When the Packers got out to California, I knew my plan wasn't working," said Fred Williamson. "Sheeit, these guys picked up the papers, read where the Packers arrived and nearly died. The Packers beat us by stepping off the airplane. Coaches were running around, drawing their X's and O's, and telling guys, 'Hey, man, get that left foot up a little higher when you run,' and 'Turn your shoulder a little to the right when you block,' and 'Tie your shoelaces in a double knot so's you won't fall and break your leg.' They had diagrams and play books and theoretical answers for everything. But they couldn't see the forest for the trees, man. This team didn't need any X's and O's. It needed confidence and somebody to say, 'Yeah, you cats gonna whip those Packers' asses. Yeah, you cats gonna be world champions.'

"I could tell the way the guys were acting toward me that they were hating me real bad around now. But nobody would challenge me physically, because I've got a black belt in karate and I knew they were intimidated by that. They weren't hating me because I was getting all the ink — and, man, was I getting *ink*. They were hating me because they were scared I was firing up the Green Bay Packers. Can you imagine that? *Firing up the Green Bay Packers.* Little ol' Fred Williamson? Boolshit. Willie Davis said to me a few nights before the game, 'Hammer, the guys are lovin' ya. They're running around practice with hammers drawn on the backs of their shirts, and they're laughing when they read the papers and when somebody makes a tackle in practice, somebody's always saying to the guy getting up, Hey, The Hammer just got ya.' I asked Willie if the Packers were fired up because of me and he said, 'Sheeit, no, they think you got some class, man. Some of those cats have been dying to express themselves for years, man, but they won't dare, not with Lombardi around.'

"I saw Buck Buchanan the next day, and he said to me, 'Damn, Rico, you're somethin' else, man.' I knew what he meant. In black talk, three or four words say a lot. He called me Rico, my nickname, and then he's saying, 'Man, you're outa your head. You're preposterous. Those Packers are going to be waiting for you, and cripple you up good.' Boolshit. Buck Buchanan's the biggest and strongest guy in the game and here he's telling me I'm somethin' else because I'm doing what he's afraid to do. *He's* afraid of opening his mouth, and *he's* afraid of saying what he really feels. They were pitiful, right down the line, every one of them. If the Packers walked into our locker room, I would expect the guys to get right down on their hands and knees and start asking them which boot they wanted licked first. I knew they had the losing attitude and I was realizin' there wasn't anything I could do about it, no matter how hard I tried. The coaches had the rest of the guys brainwashed. Even if the guys did feel like I did, even if they did have the guts to say what I said, they'd be scared that the coaches would get even with them some day, some way. Some of these guys were even walking around and preachin' about holding up the honor of the AFL. What honor, man? You tell me what honor? Stram kept brainwashing everybody by saying it's an honor to be representing our league in this, the biggest and holiest and firstest Super Bowl game ever. He made it sound like the league was doing us a favor by letting us play. Boolshit.

"I was doing the league a favor by showing up."

> LOS ANGELES, Jan. 11 (UPI) — A federal judge refused today to issue an injunction that would have prohibited a blackout in the Los Angeles area of the telecast of the Super Bowl football game on Jan. 15.
>
> District Judge William Green ruled that the regional blackout was justified on legal terms. He did say, however, that he personally felt the blackout was discriminatory against residents of southern California.
>
> The suit was filed by Alan Minter, a businessman and football fan.

From the Los Angeles Times of January 12:

> Beat The Local Blackout and See The Super Bowl Game on Home TV Tomorrow. Build Your Own Antenna From Broomsticks and Coat Hangers. Fool-Proof System. Money Refunded If It Does Not Work. Send $2 to John McNeff, Grand Prairie, Texas.

"Our game plan would not be much different from those we'd worked up all season long," said Phil Bengtson, the Packers' defensive coach. "Lombardi said that when you're winning, you don't alter your basic style of play. The first half would be devoted to probing, testing and spotting weaknesses. In the second half, we would turn loose Bart Starr and let him throw as much as he needed to. But the idea of a rout, in the sense of college mismatches, really never crossed our minds.

"We could see from films that the Kansas City defense was conscious of the deep threat whenever it faced a quarterback who could throw. But it was less than adequate on the flanks. That meant, to us, that Starr could expect to hit Dowler, Dale and McGee and, when you're capable of hitting your flankers and spread ends, the outlook for a succession of first downs is good.

"Studying the habits of their personnel, we found a few defensive linemen and a linebacker with problems of ego and eagerness that made them ripe for setting up. By showing them certain basic plays early and giving them ideas on how and where to rush, we felt we could make variations of those same plays work in the second half. That approach is no big secret or innovation, but it works especially well when age meets youth and experience meets ambition. Nothing gives a veteran lineman more hours of warm, contemplative pleasure than the thought of setting up a youngster for the big play in the third period.

"We could see indications that blitzing on both sides might make a difference as the game wore on. I advised Vince that I would not call a blitz in the first half, giving Kansas City's quarterback, Len Dawson, a

false assurance that we could capitalize on when we needed to later in the game. Dawson ran a play-action pattern of the type we rarely faced, but we felt it was particularly vulnerable to a surprise blitz. Kansas City, on the other hand, would doubtless be coming at Starr with its blitz, so we drilled our receivers in handling the man-on-man defense.

"We made one small adjustment in our thinking. Ordinarily, the coaches in any contest keep a frequency chart on the opponent for quick reference regarding 'what they'll do in this situation.' Usually a strong team goes with its successful attack, knowing that the other side has the set of statistics but saying, in effect, 'Try and stop us anyway.' We decided that since Kansas City was a total unknown, we could keep a completely uncharacteristic choice of plays as an ace in the hole to be used in the latter stages of the game if we found ourselves needing a shot in the arm. Bart had done a page or two of Kansas City's homework and he knew what the Chiefs' defense expected from him. He knew what would surprise them, and what wouldn't. Bart always was an A student."

KANSAS CITY, Jan. 14 (AP) — The Baker University Choir of Baldwin, Kan., today canceled performances scheduled for tomorrow afternoon and evening in Kansas City churches. The university said the performances were being canceled due to "lack of interest."

GREEN BAY, Jan. 14 (AP) — A patrolman from the Green Bay Police Department, scheduled for duty in the downtown section of the city tomorrow afternoon, said he did not plan to issue any parking tickets. "But if I see any cars on the street," he said, "I'll stop them and ask the driver why he isn't home watching the Packers in the Super Bowl? If he doesn't have a good reason, then I'll give him a ticket."

From the front of a church in Tomah, Wisconsin, January 14:

FIRST CONGREGATIONAL CHURCH
UNITED CHURCH OF CHRIST
Tomah, Wisconsin
WORSHIP   11:00 A.M.
WELCOME
Rev. Daniel R. Schmeichen
GO GO PACKERS GO GO

LOS ANGELES, Jan. 14 (AP) — The Super Bowl Committee announced today that 1,049 press credentials had been issued for tomorrow's game in Memorial Coliseum. The breakdown is 338 for newspaper, magazine and wire service reporters; 262 for television and radio staffs; 170

17

Quarterback Len Dawson would lead the AFL's challenge.

for photographers; 88 for press box officials; 78 for league officials; 73 for communications services, and 40 for side-line services.

From The New York Times *of January 14:*

"I plan to spend tomorrow afternoon in front of my television set," said Sen. Robert F. Kennedy (D, N.Y.) from his Hickory Hill, Virginia, home. "Vince Lombardi is an old friend of mine. He was active in the 1960 campaign. We're for Green Bay all the way."

"I'm sure it'll be a good game," said Mayor John V. Lindsay of New York City, from Gracie Mansion, "but I don't plan on watching it. I have so little time with my family that I have to take advantage of every opportunity I get. We're going to spend the afternoon playing tennis."

NEW YORK, Jan. 14 (UPI) — The National Broadcasting Company has announced that the one-minute commercials during the telecast of the Super Bowl football game tomorrow will cost each sponsor $70,000.

NEW YORK, Jan. 14 (AP) — The Columbia Broadcasting System has announced that 18 one-minute commercials during the telecasting of the Super Bowl game tomorrow will cost each sponsor $85,000.

From the Los Angeles Times *of January 14:*

The weather forecast for tomorrow afternoon: Fair and seasonably warm, with temperatures in the low to middle 70's.

"When I got up on the morning of the game, my stomach had this crazy feeling and I knew I was ready to play some football," said Curtis McClinton, fullback for the Chiefs. "I wasn't hungry, and I didn't want to talk to anybody, and I didn't even want to see anybody. I just wanted to get to the stadium, put my gear on and play.

"The ten days out here were the worst ten days of the season for me. There were too many things to adjust to — the weather, the intense practices, the seclusion, the heavy press coverage. Everything was bottled up inside of me and I was dying to let it out. I was at my peak, mentally and physically. A couple more days here and I'd have been past it. Then I would have wanted to go home and forget about the whole thing."

"When I opened my eyes that morning," said the Packers' Bob Skoronski, "I simply said to myself, 'This is it.' I had that strange feeling I always had on the morning of a game, but this time it was different. I was tense and irritable, as always, but that morning I had a feeling of desperation.

I kept telling myself, 'If we blow this one, there is no next week to get even. This is the whole season, right here, today, right now.' It was as if the Chiefs were torturing us with their presence and we had to go out and wipe them out for once and for all, like lancing a festering boil. I was desperate to get to the stadium.

"There was a fear of the unknown in me. 'How good are they?' I kept asking myself. 'Just how good?' Hell, I knew that if I was going to play opposite Doug Atkins, say, he would be capable of beating my brains out because he's done it at one time or another in the past. But Chuck Hurston and Buck Buchanan? They were mysteries, and it was bugging me pretty damn good. On top of that, I was sick and tired of practicing and I was sick and tired of living in that motel and I was sick and tired of being on edge.

"The only laughs we had all week were when we read the papers and saw what Fred Williamson had to say."

From The New York Times *of January 15:*

Before the game, Jack Whitaker of the CBS broadcasting team was telling reporters that he had stopped eating breakfast this week. "This is serious stuff," said Whitaker. "I weighed 162 at the start of the season. I wanted to be down to 155 for this game."

Outside the Coliseum, the Tiger Band from Grambling (La.) College was assembling. It was to perform at half time. Its director, Conrad Hutchinson, Jr., said, "Most bands march at a pace of 130 to 145 steps a minute. Our range is between 90 and 200. While most bands take six steps to move five yards, we use eight short ones. The strain on the marchers is so great, we don't dare allow girls in our band."

From the New York World Journal Tribune *of January 15:*

The NFL partisans showing up at the stadium had twisted emotions. Art Rooney, the Pittsburgh Steelers' owner, had sent Vince Lombardi a telegram of good will before the game, and Mrs. George Halas, Jr., arrived wearing a Packers' booster button on her coat. The NFL people were hoping the Packers would win . . . and then be seized by cholera.

From the Los Angeles Times *of January 15:*

Ten Apollo astronauts from Houston, led by Walter Schirra, were escorted into the stadium as a group and then, with diplomacy typical of a government agency, split up. Five went to sit on the Green Bay side of the field, five on the Kansas City side.

"Vince never made a big thing out of the coin toss," said Skoronski, the Packers' offensive captain. "It was the same every game. Always call

Fuzzy Thurston (63) and Jerry Kramer lead Elijah Pitts on Packer power sweep.

The cast of stars included K.C.'s Otis Taylor and Green Bay's Willie Davis.

heads and if it comes up heads always take the ball. Vince always wanted to drive it down somebody's throat before they drove it down ours.

"One of the guys once said that heads is a better percentage call because the eagle side of the coin weighed more. Because of the weight, the chances of it coming up heads were better. Now, I couldn't imagine Vince taking a coin and flipping it a couple thousand times to see if the guy was right, but he bought the idea. Willie Davis and I went through the whole season calling heads but, funny thing is, nobody ever kept score on how we did.

"Another thing Willie and I always enjoyed was the handshake after the flip. We always tried to gauge the other team's strength by the strength of the captain's handshake. If a guy shakes like his hand is a dead fish, then he's gotta be a pushover. So will his team. If he puts some muscle into it, then maybe he's gonna be trouble. Same with his club. Willie and I always gave out the most brutal handshakes we could. We'd grab the guy's hand and try to submerge it in ours, and then we'd squeeze like hell. If we could intimidate a guy at the coin flip, it was one less guy Vince would have to worry about.

"On this day the flip was held hours before the game, and we called heads and won. We elected to receive. I shook hands with Len Dawson and squeezed like hell. Then I shook with Jerry Mays, their other captain. When I turned away and ran back to the locker room, I remembered something about Mays. Vince had cut him from the Packers a few years before."

"When the guys started getting dressed, they started talking it up a little bit, you know, 'Let's get 'em' and all this boolshit," said Williamson. "But it was too late. They were just building up their courage so they could go out on the field. We were a beaten team, and I knew it.

"One of the guys said to me, 'Hey, what's it like being the Cassius Clay of football?' Trying to make conversation, you know. Boolshit. So I said to him, 'Don't lay any of that jive on me, man. I'm not the Cassius Clay of football. Cassius Clay is the Fred Williamson of boxing.' I said, 'I saw Cassius at a banquet a few months ago and he said to me, 'So you're Freddie The Hammer, huh?' And I said, 'Yeah.' And he said, 'Why, you're almost as pretty as I am.' And I said to him, 'Man, I *am* prettier'n you.' Well, that shut the guy up and he didn't open his mouth again.

"When we finally went out on the field to warm up, the Packers were looking over at me, waving and smiling. Boyd Dowler came over and said, 'Hey, Hammer, you're not going to use that thing on me, are you?' He was smiling and friendly, not fired up, and he didn't have any *im-pet-us*, which was Stram's boolshit word. So I said to him, 'Dowler, man, you catch any passes on me, you're gonna find out.' And he laughed again and went back with the rest of them. The Packers were cool, man, confident. And here we were saying high school go-get-'ems and the coaches are walking around with their clipboards, telling guys, 'Yeah, keep your head down when you run with the ball' and 'Yeah, don't forget to put some shoulder into your tackles,' and I'm saying to myself, 'Man, this is a lost cause.' So I figured, what the hell, I tried — I tried like hell — to get this team going, to get its blood pumping. Is it my fault that they're too stupid to realize it? 'My job is going to be easier,' I said to myself, 'because Old Man Lombardi over there, he's been reading the papers and he's not going to challenge me. No way. He's gonna work on Willie Mitchell over there, because Willie's scared. A couple passes in Willie's territory and Willie's gonna go to pieces. He's got some choice, Lombardi has. The Hammer on one side, a scared kid on the other. Who do you think he's going to pick on?' I was confident, man, and I was hoping the Packers made the mistake of coming my way to test me. They might have done it once, baby, but not twice.

"We went back into the locker room and put our pads on, then we came back out on the field and I was ready to kick some ass. They have this huddle on the sidelines and everybody gathers around Stram, and you can't hear a word the guy's saying, so you just jump up and down a few times and slap the guy next to you on the butt and put on a little show. That's the pregame ritual, just like the Washington Carver High School Panthers have. Then they send you out on the field, and you're eager as hell, and some announcer says, 'Ladies and Gents . . . please stand for the national anthem.' National anthem, sheeit. Here I am, my heart beating inside my head, and now I gotta turn everything off and stand there listening to some cat sing about the land of the free and the home of the brave. The whole thing is boolshit. No way you can turn the enthusiasm on and off. By the time the cat stops singing, you're empty again. I'm saying to myself, 'Why don't they play it after the game . . . yeah, why don't they play it after the game and see how many of these patriots are gonna stay around.' I'm standing out there on the field, and I'm looking down at the grass, and I'm not even listening, because I'm thinking to myself, 'Next they're gonna bring out the Reverend Jones from the local Baptist Church, and he's gonna bless our daily bread and ask the Good Lord to protect all these fine young men on the field of combat today.' It's more boolshit. All the Reverend Jones cares about is getting a free ticket to the game."

> *GREEN BAY, Jan. 15 (UPI) — The only person spotted walking down a street in the business section of this city today at 2:05 p.m., was a policeman. He was carrying a nightstick in his left hand, a transistor radio in his right.*

Just before the kickoff, after the field had been cleared of 313 musi-

THE OPENING MATCHUPS

GREEN BAY ON OFFENSE

No.	Player	Ht.	Wt.	Pos.
84	Carroll Dale	6-4	200	WR
86	Boyd Dowler	6-5	225	WR
81	Marv Fleming	6-4	235	TE
75	Forrest Gregg	6-4	250	RT
64	Jerry Kramer	6-3	245	RG
50	Bill Curry	6-2	235	C
63	Fred Thurston	6-1	245	LG
70	Bob Skoronski	6-3	250	LT
15	Bart Starr	6-1	200	QB
22	Elijah Pitts	6-1	205	RB
31	Jim Taylor	6-0	215	FB

KANSAS CITY ON DEFENSE

No.	Player	Ht.	Wt.	Pos.
22	Willie Mitchell	6-1	185	RCB
24	Fred Williamson	6-3	209	LCB
20	Bobby Hunt	6-1	193	SS
75	Jerry Mays	6-4	225	LE
58	Andy Rice	6-2	260	LT
69	Sherrill Headrick	6-2	240	MLB
86	Buck Buchanan	6-7	287	RT
85	Chuck Hurston	6-6	240	RE
42	John Robinson	6-1	205	FS
78	Bobby Bell	6-4	228	LLB
55	E. J. Holub	6-4	236	RLB

KANSAS CITY ON OFFENSE

No.	Player	Ht.	Wt.	Pos.
88	Chris Burford	6-3	220	WR
89	Otis Taylor	6-2	211	WR
84	Fred Arbanas	6-3	240	TE
73	Dave Hill	6-5	264	RT
64	Curt Merz	6-4	267	RG
66	Wayne Frazier	6-3	245	C
71	Ed Budde	6-5	260	LG
77	Jim Tyrer	6-6	292	LT
16	Len Dawson	6-0	190	QB
21	Mike Garrett	5-9	155	RB
32	Curtis McClinton	6-3	222	FB

GREEN BAY ON DEFENSE

No.	Player	Ht.	Wt.	Pos.
26	Herb Adderley	6-0	210	RCB
21	Bob Jeter	6-1	205	LCB
40	Tom Brown	6-1	190	SS
87	Willie Davis	6-3	245	LE
77	Ron Kostelnik	6-4	260	LT
66	Ray Nitschke	6-3	240	MLB
74	Henry Jordan	6-3	250	RT
82	Lionel Aldridge	6-4	245	RE
24	Willie Wood	5-10	190	FS
89	Dave Robinson	6-3	245	LLB
60	Lee Roy Caffey	6-3	250	RLB

cians, 80 baton-twirlers, several glee clubs, a few floats and enough photographers to cover the second coming of Amos Alonzo Stagg — if not of Pop Warner himself — 4,000 pigeons were released into the air. Symbolically, perhaps, they crashed into each other, wings flapping wildly, and then, at an altitude of 150 feet, before they could make the crowd under them squirm with thoughts of moistened coiffures, they vanished quickly, like burglars into the night, leaving center stage to the sole possession of Kansas City's kicker, Mike Mercer.

On the second play of the game, the Packers' Elijah Pitts — Paul Hornung's replacement — ran a play around left end. When Boyd Dowler attempted to block out E. J. Holub, a Kansas City linebacker, he reinjured a shoulder and was forced to leave the game. Max McGee, thirty-four years old, who was as adept at reading defensive alignments as he was at reading neon signs that flickered and bubbled, replaced him.

The night before the game, McGee and Hornung, who were roommates on the road, spent a rather uncharacteristic evening. They talked to each other. Hornung, with a pinched nerve in his neck, sensed that he would never play in another football game. McGee was less despondent. He sensed that he would not play in this game.

In the locker room before the game, McGee dressed next to Hornung and said to him, "I wonder if I'll get a chance to play in this thing. I guess it's me if Dowler gets hurt again, but you know how little I've played all year. I just don't know about my legs. I know I can beat the pants off the guys in their backfield, but I don't know if the legs will hold up."

But after nine minutes of rather uneventful play, it was McGee who became the first player to score a touchdown in the Super Bowl. He caught a flank pass from Starr and, like an aging gazelle, outran the secondary into the end zone. The play covered thirty-seven yards, and with Chandler's extra point the Packers had a 7–0 lead.

Early in the second period, Dawson, using play-action passes, snapped Kansas City out of its sleepwalk. He was using Mike Garrett as a safety-valve receiver and threw to him often because Green Bay had his primary receivers covered. But several dumped passes — with Garrett's help — moved the Chiefs to the Green Bay 7-yard line.

"Dawson called a 'Right 55, Lead Pass,'" said Curtis McClinton, "which was my play. I had to get myself into the end zone and Dawson would lead me with the pass. Hopefully, the ball and my chest would arrive at a certain point at the same time. It wasn't a surprising call, because we'd used it a lot during the year when we were close. I got into the end zone all right, without much trouble at all, in fact, and Dawson was right on the button. 'Damn,' I said to myself as I caught the ball, 'touchdown.' When Mercer kicked the extra point to tie it up, I jumped up and down on the

25

Bart Starr knew what to expect from the Chiefs' Buck Buchanan (86).

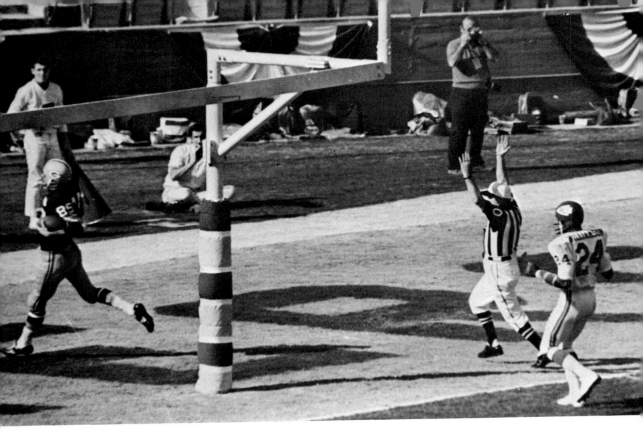

Max McGee didn't expect to play, much less score, the first TD.

Jim Taylor was Green Bay's short-yardage specialist.

Defenders Ray Nitschke (66) and Willie Wood close in on Bert Coan.

sidelines and I was yelling, 'We did it, we did it. Now let's do it again.' "

Right after the Kansas City touchdown, the Packers marched seventy-three yards with the solemnity of hangmen poised for the pull. In a dozen plays they made it to the Chiefs' 14-yard line, then pulled the lever and the trapdoor creaked. Starr called for a power sweep, and Thurston and Kramer led Taylor into the end zone as assuredly as a man leads his dog to the curb. Chandler's kick made it 14–7, Green Bay.

"It was a scene out of a 1962 newsreel," said Bengtson. "That touchdown did more than just put us ahead. It put us on the way to victory. Not only did we move steadily on the ground, but a pass to Dale in the end zone, which was nullified by a penalty, was made possible when we suckered a corner back into going for the fake to Taylor and letting Dale slip by him. Our homework was paying off. Bart established that he could pick away at the defensive backs, hitting his ends for ten- and fifteen-yarders. They were our bread-and-butter plays. They were working. We didn't have to get tricky."

Early in the third quarter, Willie Davis and Henry Jordan put the pass rush on Dawson, and Willie Wood intercepted one of his passes and returned it to the Kansas City 5-yard line. From there, Pitts went into the end zone, doing a pirouette over fallen bodies. Chandler's kick put Green Bay ahead, 21–10.

"That was the game, right there," said Fred Williamson. "The Chiefs quit after the interception, and when Pitts went in, hell, about eight guys touched him and slapped at him and he never even broke stride. We should have gone home, then, before it got messy. I'd be standing on the sidelines, watching the offense try to move the ball, and I knew it was hopeless. Nobody was thinking. Hell, Adderley was playing ten to twelve yards off Otis Taylor, and Dawson wasn't throwing to Otis, not at all. That's how we got to the Super Bowl in the first place — Dawson throwing to Otis. Otis should have been the star of the game, because he was the best receiver on the field. He made one catch in the first half that was out of this world, man. Adderley wasn't taking any chances with him. He knew that once Otis got behind him, it was all over. But Otis, man, he was in the doghouse to start with. He blew the flight from Kansas City and flew out on his own the same night. He made it to practice on time, but ol' Stram put it to him. Fined him a couple hundred. When a guy's in the coach's doghouse, a lot of the other guys won't have anything to do with him, like he's carrying the plague or something."

In the third period, McGee's aching legs carried him from the Kansas City 13 to five yards deep in the end zone. Starr passed to him, Chandler

Old Man McGee scores his second touchdown.

kicked the extra point and the Packers went into the last quarter with a 28–10 lead.

"Early in the last quarter, I was aching for some action," said Williamson. "Ol' Lombardi, he didn't send anything my way all day. I put one hammer to Dale and that was it. So I saw this Packer sweep coming, with Anderson carrying, and I said to myself, 'Get that muthah.' This kid Gillingham was leading the sweep and I was overanxious, emotional, and I made a big mistake. I went into him, head first, and I caught his knee right on the forehead. The next thing I knew I was lying on a stretcher on the sidelines looking up at all that blue. I asked somebody, 'What the hell happened?' And he said, 'You got knocked out cold.' Man, was I embarrassed."

"It was funny as hell," said Gillingham. "Nobody was out to get Williamson, nobody was mad at him at all. In fact, we thought the guy was pretty funny. But it was ironic seeing him getting carried off the field. I could imagine everybody in the stands saying, 'Well, there goes The Hammer, the big mouth. The Packers got him.' That wasn't the case at all. The Packers didn't get him. He got himself.

"I had gone into the game as Thurston's replacement and I pulled out to lead the sweep, with Donny Anderson carrying behind me. I saw Williamson coming at me like a wild man and I knew he was going to try to take me out of the play, leaving Anderson unprotected for somebody else. To my surprise, he came barreling at me real low and I simply picked my knee up a little and he caught it flush on the head. Then Anderson went over the top and all three of us just lay there for a while. Donny and I got up slowly, and Williamson didn't get up at all.

"He had a lot of momentum going for him, because my knee hurt like hell after, and Donny had to leave the game to get his bearings."

By now the Chiefs were floundering with all the eloquence of men drowning. But the Packers added one more touchdown, sending Pitts over from a yard out. Chandler's fifth extra point made it 35–10, where it stood until the last anticlimactic tick of the clock.

"Kansas City has a good team," said Vince Lombardi, surrounded by newsmen outside the Packer dressing room after the game. "But it doesn't compare with some of the teams in the NFL. Dallas is a better team. That's what you want me to say, isn't it? There. I've said it."

"Vince came around after the game and gave everybody a bear hug and a fierce handshake," said Skoronski. "That was the extent of the cele-

31

The Chiefs had their problems bringing down Donny Anderson.

bration in the locker room. But deep down inside, where it really counted, the joy was indescribable. It's a moment I'll never be able to recapture for as long as I live."

"I felt like one of the losers at Pompeii," said McClinton. "I was overwhelmed by the feeling that there would never be another chance, that there would never be another Super Bowl game or another football season. It was like being on a deathbed. Everything you've accomplished up to that point didn't mean a damn thing anymore.

"Never before had I felt like such a loser. There was no way we could tell ourselves we played a fine game; we hadn't. The Packers exposed our weaknesses to the world. They picked apart our defense, they stopped our offense, they demoralized us. There was nothing in this game that indicated it could have gone either way.

"Leaving the stadium that night, I could not convince myself that there would be another season, another big game, another Super Bowl. The despair of it all blighted my senses."

"A few weeks after we returned to Green Bay, I got a call from Vince," said Skoronski. "He said, 'Well, are you going to help me design the rings or aren't you?' I said, 'Yes, coach. When do you want to see me?' He said, 'Soon as possible.' I worked for a company in the off-season that was manufacturing the rings we were going to receive for winning the game, and Vince wanted to design them himself.

"We got together, and Vince was bubbling over with ideas. We went back and forth, back and forth. Finally, I decided to let him handle it all. He wanted half a globe on the top of the ring, to symbolize our being champions of the entire world. I said, 'Yeah, I like that.' And he wanted the word 'Desire' up there on top, too. He said that for all the words he used in football, 'Desire' seemed to sum up his philosophy best. Again I agreed with him.

"During those couple days with Vince, working on the rings, I recaptured some of the jubilation I had felt right after winning the game. Maybe it was being around Vince that did it. When I went back to work, the feeling vanished. There was something about Vince that brought out a feeling of pride in a player. It was as if he were saying, 'Look at you. You've accomplished something in your lifetime. How many people accomplish anything?' "

"I was home in California, wiping out the memories," said Fred Williamson, "and I was thinking that maybe I wanted to retire from football. Everybody was dumping the loss on me. They were saying, 'If

32

Max McGee had the last laugh.

Williamson had kept his mouth shut, maybe we would have won.' And the sportswriters, they didn't come around anymore. They were busy writing, 'Yeah, the Packers took care of The Hammer. They knocked him out of the game.' What boolshit. I was getting the rap. I was the fall guy. But nobody — man, nobody — came around and told the real story. They figured Fred Williamson was a perfect dumping ground, so let's dump the whole thing on him and now let's start thinking about the Pro Bowl and the draft and, yeah, the baseball season.

"Football was becoming a big bore and I was asking myself, 'Are you going to go through all that again? The training camp, the coaches, the X's and O's?' I was thinking that maybe I'd like to be an actor, to expand myself instead of staying the same. It all came to a head one day when I was going through my mail and there, in this official envelope, was my Super Bowl check. 'Oh well,' I said, 'seventy-five hundred. Not bad for one little ol' game.' Well, I opened the envelope and pulled out the check, and when I looked at it my eyeballs came protruding out of my head about a foot, like that guy's in the comic strips. There it was, staring right back at me — four, five, zee-ro, zee-ro. Forty-five hundred dollars, and change, after taxes. I said to myself, 'So this is what you clear from the multimillion-dollar, Super, Super, Super Bowl? Forty-five hundred dollars? Boolshit.' "

Vince Lombardi: Design for triumph.

MAN FOR MAN

Participants — Oakland Raiders, champions of the American Football League, and Green Bay Packers, champions of the National Football League.

Date — January 14, 1968.

Site — Orange Bowl Stadium, Miami, Florida.

Time — 3:05 P.M., EST.

Attendance — 75,546.

Radio and Television — Columbia Broadcasting System (TV and Radio).

Regular-Season Records — Oakland, 13-1; Green Bay, 9-4-1.

Playoff Records — Oakland defeated Houston Oilers, 40-7, for AFL title; Green Bay defeated Dallas Cowboys, 21-17, for NFL title.

Players' Shares — $15,000 to each member of winning team; $7,500 to each member of losing team.

Gate Receipts — Estimated $750,000.

Radio-TV Receipts — $2,500,000.

Officials — Referee, Jack Vest, AFL; Umpire, Ralph Morcroft, NFL; Linesman, Tony Vetri, AFL; Back Judge, Stan Javie, NFL; Field Judge, Bob Bauer, AFL; Line Judge, Bruce Alford, NFL.

Coaches — John Rauch, Oakland; Vince Lombardi, Green Bay.

BOCA RATON, Fla., Jan. 4 (AP) — The Oakland Raiders, champions of the American Football League, arrived here today to begin training for the Super Bowl game against the Green Bay Packers on Jan. 14 in Miami.

From News Dispatches of January 4:

The Oakland Raiders, unlike most teams preparing for a big game, will not have closed-door practices. There are no doors to close. The Raiders have been practicing on a field in the far corner of the campus of St. Andrew's Boys School in Boca Raton, a private Roman Catholic institution. There is only one access road leading to the practice field and the Raiders have stationed uniformed guards at the gate to bar everyone but authorized personnel. Security, needless to say, is stringent. The only exposed area of the field is a swamp that lies soggily beyond the far sideline. The swamp is populated by alligators and water moccasins.

Fred Biletnikoff, wide receiver for the Oakland Raiders, arrived today at the team's practice field at St. Andrew's Boys School in Boca Raton. After scanning the landscape, he said he would not be running any sideline patterns.

From The New York Times *of January 5:*

Al Davis, managing general partner of the Oakland Raiders, said today that "the great snow job" had begun.

"If we play like we did against Houston (in the AFL championship game), there is no reason why we can't beat the best," said Daryle Lamonica, the Raider quarterback, after Oakland's first workout. "If we do beat the best, then we'll have to be considered the best. Some people have compared me with Bart Starr. I don't copy anyone, although I do admire Starr. But I consider it a real privilege to play against the man who is rated tops in the business."

"This is the best team I've ever played on," said George Blanda, forty years old, the Raiders' kicking specialist, "and I've played on eighteen of 'em. This team is not going to roll over and play dead. We're not awed by the Packers. We'll give a good account of ourselves."

"This team has a great deal of confidence," said John Rauch, the Raiders' coach. "It has grown in confidence from week to week. The men on this team, I am sure, will respond to one more challenge, like taking on the very best team in all of football."

"Imagine," said Davis, "the li'l ol' Raiders on the same field with the Green Bay Packers. *Imagine . . .*"

GREEN BAY, Jan. 5 (UPI) — The Green Bay Packers held a closed practice session here yesterday after jeeps with brushes had swept away four inches of snow off the field. The temperature was four degrees above zero. The Packers plan to continue practicing here until Sunday, when they will fly to Fort Lauderdale, Fla.

"The Packers' number is fourteen," said Demetrius Synodinus of Steubenville, Ohio, alias Jimmy (The Greek) Snyder, from his Information Unlimited office in Las Vegas, Nevada. "It's a strong fourteen, at that. I don't just pick numbers out of the thin air. I analyze both teams and translate their strengths or weaknesses into the language of points.

"In this game, the team speeds will be equal, so there are no points involved there. But I had to give Bart Starr two points over Daryle Lamonica at quarterback. You can't call Lamonica a great quarterback off of one big year. He's got to do it year after year, like Starr has. You don't know, either, if Lamonica is going to hold up in a big game like this. Starr has.

"On the defensive front four, it's another two-point edge for the Packers. They have four fine pass-rushers, and the Raiders have only two — Tom Keating and Ike Lassiter. At middle linebacker, Ray Nitschke is worth three points. The kid the Raiders got, Dan Conners, is good, too. He's a one-point player, but that's a two-point difference in Nitschke's favor.

"In the defensive backfield, the Packers have a big edge, four points, I'd say. Herb Adderley, Bob Jeter and Willie Wood are the best. The Raiders don't have defensive backs in that class. Look at what the Jets did to them with George Sauer and Don Maynard.

"The Packers get two points for their receivers, too. Boyd Dowler and Carroll Dale, they catch the ball against everybody. That's twelve points for the Packers, so far, and then you've got to give them three more points for the intangibles — the coach, Lombardi, is a big intangible, and so is their record in the big games.

"That's a total of fifteen points for the Packers. But take away one because of George Blanda. He's a better place-kicker than Don Chandler. You've got to give the Raiders a point for him. That brings it down to fourteen points. That number should hold up. I doubt if it will drop much below thirteen and a half, if it drops at all. The intangibles are too much in the Packers' favor.

"Myself, I look for the Packers to play a conservative first half. Lombardi will want to find out who's working on who, and his game plan for the second half should be something. That's how they beat Kansas City last year — in the second half — and that's when the Raiders will be in real trouble."

> NEW YORK, Jan. 5 (UPI) — Daryle Lamonica of the Oakland Raiders, who went from the No. 2 quarterback on the No. 2 team to the No. 1 quarterback on the No. 1 team in one season, was chosen today as the United Press International Player of the Year in the American Football League. Lamonica received 22 votes from 27 writers, three from each league city. Hewritt Dixon of Oakland was second in the balloting with three votes, and John Hadl of the San Diego Chargers and Joe Namath of the New York Jets were tied for third with one vote each. Lamonica was the backup quarterback to Jack Kemp last season with the Buffalo Bills, AFL runners-up.

"I was shocked to my teeth when I first heard that the Bills had traded me to Oakland," said Lamonica in the lobby of the Raiders' motel in Boca Raton. "I had a long talk with Joel Collier, the Bills' coach, after the season ended and he assured me that I would be getting an even chance to be the No. 1 quarterback in training camp the following summer.

"I didn't hear about the trade until I came home from hunting the night it happened. Then I was floored. But the day turned out all right. I shot a thirty-five-pound bobcat with a .22-caliber pistol, and named the bobcat 'Raider.' "

"We had our eye on Lamonica for a long time," said Rauch. "He had everything we wanted in a quarterback. He had more experience than most backup quarterbacks and he was tall enough and heavy enough and sturdy enough. He became our leader immediately and established our esprit de corps.

"Geography helped speed his development. He lives in Fresno, and I live in Oakland, a drive of a little more than two hours. So, we would get together every day for a couple of weeks at a time and go over movies of our offense. I'd stop the projector before each play and explain what each call would be and why. It was a cram course in strategic theories. He learned fast.

"There are some people who say that our offense is too complicated. I don't agree with any of them. I think it's similar to mastering a foreign language. It may be tough at first, but the more fluent one gets, the easier it is. Lamonica is fluent, I can tell you that."

"The Packers and the Bills drafted me after my senior season at Notre Dame," said Lamonica. "I really didn't give much thought to signing with the Packers. I wanted to play right away. Besides, they drafted me on the thirteenth round."

> *GREEN BAY, Jan. 7 (AP) — About 250 fans assembled today at the wind-swept airport with temperatures ten degrees below zero to cheer the Green Bay Packers as they departed on a charter flight for Fort Lauderdale, Fla. The Packers left behind four inches of snow. They worked out lightly Friday in a high school gymnasium and went through even lighter drills yesterday. But Coach Vince Lombardi said that a full week of training has been scheduled this week in Florida. The temperature here has not been above the freezing point for two weeks.*

> *FORT LAUDERDALE, Jan. 7 (UPI) — The Green Bay Packers arrived here tonight to begin their training for the Super Bowl game amid recurring reports that Vince Lombardi would retire as head coach after the game and become the team's full-time general manager. Phil Bengtson, his defensive coach, is reported to have agreed to become Lombardi's successor as head coach.*

"The rumors started during the summer," said Bengtson, "and some of them were utterly ridiculous, not to mention unfounded. During the season, a Chicago columnist with a few spare inches of space to fill said that I would be the successor to Norm Van Brocklin as head coach of the Minnesota Vikings, and that Van Brocklin would come to Green Bay as Lombardi's top assistant. But no team had contacted me for a couple of years. Everybody knew that it would have taken an extremely attractive offer to lure me away from the Packers. Lombardi squelched the rumor for once and for all, and I told the press that I intended to stay right where I was.

"But after that episode, I seemed to have developed an automatic identification in the press: 'Vince Lombardi's heir apparent, Phil Bengtson.' I did nothing to foster it, and Lombardi never once hinted at it. But it would not die. Some columnists and fans managed to convince themselves that Lombardi and I spent most of our spare time up in the throne room discussing the future, but nothing could be further from the truth. The fact is that Lombardi and I never mixed much socially, rarely talked about high-level positions of power at any length, and spent very little time speculating on our coaching careers together. There simply was no time for politics from June to January. Every year around February 15, just before I left for my annual vacation in Arizona, Vince would stick his head in my office and ask me some mundane question like, 'How many sheets of poster board will you need to set up your depth charts for next year?' I would say, 'About six.' Then we would both smile. Something unspoken carried the message that we intended to work together for another year."

"Vince was a lot different going into the Super Bowl this year than he was last year," said Don Chandler, the Green Bay place-kicker. "Last year he never smiled and it was like we were in training camp. This year he smiles once in a while . . . and he allowed us to bring our wives."

"If there is one thing wrong with football," Lombardi said, as he talked with reporters upon arriving at the Gault Ocean Mile Motel in Fort Lauderdale, "it's the length of the season. It's too long. The regular season should never end as late as December 31. There are just too many games — and not enough players. I'd like to see the roster limit raised from forty players to forty-three or even forty-five. We need more bodies. This is our twenty-third game of the season."

From The New York Times *of January 8:*

> Even if you have a color television set, you will be watching the Super Bowl game in black and white. The Oakland Raiders will be wearing black jerseys on Sunday, the Green Bay Packers white ones.

> *MIAMI, Jan. 8 (AP)— The Super Bowl game was reported sold out today, assuring the Green Bay Packers and the Oakland Raiders of more than 70,000 spectators for their Jan. 14 contest in the Orange Bowl.*

From News Dispatches of January 8:

Al Davis, managing general partner of the Oakland Raiders, confirmed today that his team's pregame approach was one of formal flattery. He said that anyone desiring details should contact Fresco Thompson, vice-president of the Los Angeles Dodgers baseball team. Davis said that Thompson was an expert in the field.

Thompson, when contacted in Los Angeles, said: "I was captain of the old Phillies team that was baseball's worst team for years. I learned then that it doesn't pay to get your opponents mad at you unnecessarily. In my day, the Yankees showed how it could be done. They always inquired about the other guy's health and the welfare of his wife and kids. Then they'd go out and beat the guy's brains out, but they were so nice about it that it seemed painless.

"But the Chicago Cubs of that era were downright nasty. They snarled at everyone and they insulted us the most, riding us as the worst collection of clowns ever assembled. One September, they came to town with the pennant almost won. But they got us so mad that we played over our heads and knocked them out of it. I learned then to let sleeping dogs lie. It keeps them harmless."

"They say I'm a wild man, an animal, a bloodthirsty savage," said Ben Davidson, six-foot-seven, 265-pound defensive right end for the Raiders. "They say I broke Joe Namath's cheekbone for no reason and that I enjoy hurting people. Now, every time they even suspect me of being too rough, they nail me with a fifteen-yard penalty. But I was pretty well beat up myself after that Jets game, so maybe I should start complaining. But, as befits my lower position, I just sit in the whirlpool and don't say a word.

"All this nonsense about intimidating quarterbacks is just that — nonsense. You can't intimidate a quarterback and make him afraid of you. Hell, these guys play every week and they don't scare. They have to concentrate on the receiver anyway. I think they feel the pressure, but they don't shake in their shoes out of fear.

"Myself, I'm looking for job security. So there are times when I just won't put up with a defensive guy holding me. He's using an illegal tactic to put my job in jeopardy. When a guy won't stop holding, you have to resort to illegal tactics yourself. What kind of illegal tactics? Kick him. Next time he'll think twice."

"I remember Ben when he was with the Packers," said Cherry Starr, sunning herself by the pool at the Gault Ocean Mile Motel. "He was a very nice man and we all liked him. He didn't have a mustache then, but that doesn't matter, I guess. He was friendly with Bart and once in a while he'd come over to the house and borrow something. One day he came over to return a pen. He was wearing this big shaggy sweater that his wife had

knit for him when he came to the door.

"Our dog is a good watchdog, and a very brave dog. But she took one look at Ben and ran howling under the bed."

"I remember Davidson," said Henry Jordan, the Packers' defensive right tackle. "We just called him 'Big Ben' in those days. The only specific thing I recall about him was the day he showed up. He arrived at the practice field driving one of those little Porsche sports cars."

"My father wore a mustache and I haven't been able to lick him yet," said Lombardi, when asked about Davidson.

"You won't believe this," said Rauch after the Raiders' workout at St. Andrew's School in Boca Raton, "but I actually played in a game against one of my players. It was in 1948. I was the quarterback at the University of Georgia. We played Kentucky, and who do you think was the quarterback? Blanda, over there. We were both seniors. No, I won't tell you the score."

> *FORT LAUDERDALE, Jan. 8 (UPI) — Vince Lombardi called the Oakland Raiders a fine team today, but said his Green Bay Packers were physically and mentally ready for Sunday's Super Bowl game in Miami. The Packers looked sharp in a brisk loosening-up drill in balmy weather. They ran through offensive signals against the defensive unit in the last practice open to the public. Contact work starts tomorrow.*

> *FORT LAUDERDALE, Jan. 10 (AP) — The Green Bay Packers went through a two-hour closed practice workout today and Coach Vince Lombardi said that he was pleased with the team's performance. "We went a little longer than usual," Lombardi said, "because I felt we needed it. We were still a little rusty today."*

"People call the American Football League a 'junior league,'" said Lombardi before retiring to the Governor's Suite for the night. "It may be a 'junior league' in terms of years, but I don't think there is a difference between eight years and forty years in our business. You get to be a pretty good veteran in eight years.

"I've studied movies of the Raiders in their last three games against Houston, Buffalo and the New York Jets. I would have preferred to have had a choice in exchanging pictures of any three games, but they insisted on the last three and I didn't argue. It shows that I'm not as unreasonable

Oakland's Big Ben Davidson was once with the Packers.

It had been a great year for Oakland quarterback Daryle Lamonica.

Now it was Gale Gillingham leading Travis Williams on the Packer power sweep.

as everyone thinks I am.

"I would like to say for the record that I am as proud of this team as any I've ever coached. Any club that could get this far while losing men like Hornung, Taylor, Pitts and Grabowski has to be special in my estimation. We made it here, mind you, with two fullbacks nobody else wanted, Chuck Mercein and Ben Wilson.

"As for the weather, I don't think it will make one bit of difference. Weather is a state of mind."

"Wally Cruice, our chief scout, kept telling us that Oakland was a team with a great many Packer and Wisconsin ties," said Phil Bengtson. "He said that it was bound to give the Raiders emotional fuel. He said that their star back, Pete Banaszak, was from Crivitz, Wisconsin, and their center, Jim Otto, was from Wausau. Their quarterback, Daryle Lamonica, was a draft choice of the Packers in 1963, and on defense, Ben Davidson and Howie Williams once played for the Packers. And there was George Blanda, whose familiarity with us dated back to his days as the right arm of Papa Bear Halas.

"But none of the information required any adjustments, as far as Lombardi was concerned. He was more concerned about the Oakland defense. 'The Angry Eleven,' it called itself. Cruice said it was a light, fast outfit that stunted, blitzed and moved around, showing a different defense on every play. They had succeeded all season long in confusing AFL offenses by varying the positioning of their line and linebackers. The defensive backs, Cruice said, reacted with great speed and had been known to snatch the ball right out of the hands of unwary would-be receivers.

"Vince devoured all the information, but we could sense that there was something else on his mind, something that went beyond the Oakland defense or Pete Banaszak's ties with Crivitz. All week long, Vince had been hounded by reporters to confirm or deny rumors of his retirement from coaching. Vince was smilingly noncommittal about it — even cagey — at first. But soon it began to wear on him and he cut off all inquiries. He was telling everyone now that when the season ended he was going to take 'a long, hard look at Vince Lombardi.'

"But as the week wore on, the players began to sense something. It began to look like Packer Old Home Week in Miami, with former players, including Paul Hornung, on hand. There were former Lombardi assistants coming around like never before, and a lot of Green Bay expatriates who were combining a Florida vacation with a renewal of old loyalties. After the last practice session on Friday, Vince called the team together.

" 'I want to say, first of all, that we all know we can win on Sunday. We are old hands at this game, but we also know that we will have to work harder

than ever without letting up for one minute. I . . .' There was a brief pause, and a few heads moved slightly to see if there was a slight catch in the usually strong, husky Lombardi voice. 'I . . . want to tell you how very proud I am of . . . of all of you. I have told you before that you are the finest team in all of professional football. It's been a long season and Sunday . . . may be the last time we are all together. Let's make it a good game, a game we can all be proud of.' By now most everyone was looking down and away. They did not have to see his face to know that there were tears in his eyes. They knew, because every eye in the room was moist and every throat was parched dry."

NEW YORK, Jan. 12 (AP) — The Columbia Broadcasting System said today that it estimates its telecast of the Super Bowl game on Sunday will have an audience of 50 million viewers. CBS is handling network coverage of the game exclusively this year. Last year, both CBS and the National Broadcasting Company televised it.

From News Dispatches of January 12:

Gene Upshaw, offensive left guard of the Oakland Raiders, asked a reporter what year it was. The reporter said, "Nineteen sixty-eight." Upshaw said, "Good. I got married on Dec. 30, and I played in the AFL title game on Dec. 31. Just want to make sure I'm in the right year."

A reporter asked Daryle Lamonica, Oakland quarterback, what keeps him from scrambling. "Two things," answered Lamonica. "Fear and common sense."

John Rauch, coach of the Oakland Raiders, continued his soft-spoken approach to Sunday's game in a brief meeting with reporters at his team's quarters in Boca Raton. When asked about the Packers, Rauch said, "Beating the Packers is always in the realm of possibility. We'll go into the game with the same confidence we've had all season long. To tell you the truth, we'd rather play the Packers than anybody because they represent the best of their league, the best for three years."

Paul Hornung, driving a multicolored jalopy, has been visiting his old teammates all week. He revealed today how strong Vince Lombardi's hold is on his former players, even after they have retired, as Hornung did this year. "I had a dream the other night that I came by and sneaked Max McGee out after hours," said Hornung. "Vinnie found out about it. Damned if he didn't fine me five hundred bucks, even though I was no longer with the team. The thing that woke me up was that I dreamed I paid the fine."

The ratings of pro football teams and players has always been a tricky

49

Al Davis was the driving force behind Oakland.

business, leading to disagreements that are rarely settled. Until now there has been no adequate standard of measurement. But a fellow in Albuquerque has come up with something he calls "The Retailer Rating and Discounter Desperation Poll." Last week he poked around in the department stores and found that:

The "Johnny Unitas Official Football," which started the season at $7.20, has dropped to a sale price of $3.88.

The "Gale Sayers" is holding at $5.79.

The "Don Meredith" tops all at $6.95.

The "Fran Tarkenton" has been marked down to $1.99.

The "Paul Hornung" can be had for one book of green stamps.

From The New York Times *of January 12:*

"The game comes at an opportune time for the hotels," a spokesman for the Miami Beach Chamber of Commerce told United Press International today. "They do a big business between Christmas and New Year's Day, and then they have a lull from Jan. 1 to Jan. 15. So this game is just perfect for us. The Carillon Hotel, one of the big ones on the ocean, is sold out at this time of year for the first time since it was built.

"Our area is getting heavy promotion in newspapers and on television. People up north will look out their windows and see snow in the driveway and a thermometer showing the temperature at zero. Then they will tune in the Super Bowl game and see sunshine and girls in summer dresses. Then — we hope — they will come on down and spend some money."

Eastern Airlines said that 900 to 1,000 people flew to Miami Beach from New York, Cleveland, Detroit, Chicago and St. Louis on special package tours arranged by the airline.

Green Bay Packer fans chartered 10 planes carrying about 100 people each to Miami Beach. The Green Bay Chamber of Commerce has built a display at the Miami airport at which it is giving away samples of Wisconsin cheese and literature telling of life in Wisconsin, generally, and Green Bay, particularly. "The cheese," a spokesman said, "is going faster than the literature."

Jim Wilson, vice-president of Restaurant and Waldorf Associates, Inc., will be caterer for the Super Bowl, as he has been for all 34 of the football games played at the Orange Bowl this season. His company also owns such restaurants as The Forum of the Twelve Caesars, the Four Seasons and Mama Leone's in New York City.

Wilson said that the capacity crowd of 75,546 would consume 40,000 Zum Zums (a smoke-cured frankfurter), bratwursts and hot dogs. If the wursts were strung together, they would cover 5,550 yards, or more than the Packers and the Raiders gained all season combined.

"When I got to training camp, I was pretty nervous," said Travis

Corner back Herb Adderley was a key to the Packer defense.

Williams, in his first season as a running back for the Packers, after a work-out at Fort Lauderdale Stadium. "I didn't do much at Arizona State the last couple years and I was a fourth-round pick. There wasn't any big pressure on me to make it. No big bonuses, or anything like that. I guess I put the pressure on myself. The result was, every time I got the ball, I dropped it. I must've set some kinda record in practice for fumbles by a running back.

"One day, Lombardi called me aside and said, 'We're gonna have to do something about you.' He told me to carry a football everywhere I went — on the field, in the locker room, to meals and even to the game movies. He said he never wanted to see me without a football in my hands. Zeke Bratkowski even made a handle for me out of adhesive tape so I could carry it easier.

"I carried the damn football every minute of the day. I wasn't taking any chances. I never knew when I might run into him."

> *FORT LAUDERDALE, Jan. 13 (UPI) — The Green Bay Packers yesterday added Dick Capp, a 23-year-old, 238-pound linebacker, to their roster. Capp, from Boston College, was released by the Boston Patriots of the American Football League in the summer of 1966.*

"I went to Boston College on a basketball scholarship," said Capp. "But I knew in my junior year that I wouldn't be good enough to play for Bob Cousy. So I went out for football. I was a fair-to-good college player — no honors, no all-anything, nothing like that. The Patriots drafted me in the fifteenth round and I played in one preseason game against Oakland. I did poorly and wasn't surprised when they cut me.

"Funny thing, my parents gave me and my sister everything when we were kids and they didn't have much to give — we grew up in Portland, Maine, and my father was a newspaper distributor — so, this Christmas, my sister and I decided to give them something — a trip to Florida on us.

"My folks are down here now, and they've never been any place before in their entire lives. I got them tickets to the game, but I never dreamed in my wildest dreams that I'd be playing in it . . . with the Packers, no less."

From News Dispatches of January 13:

Of 36 pro football players vacationing in the Miami area on the eve of the Super Bowl game, 30 of them picked the Green Bay Packers to defeat the Oakland Raiders.

Said Joe Namath, quarterback for the New York Jets: "Green Bay is just better all-around. The Packers are one of football's great teams, probably the best ever."

Tucker Frederickson, running back for the New York Giants, said: "Green Bay by 28–14."

> *MIAMI BEACH, Jan. 14 (AP) — John Rauch, coach of the Oakland Raiders, received a telegram this morning, a few hours before the start of the Super Bowl game against the Green Bay Packers. The telegram, from Boston, read: "Here is the play that will win the game for you — send Fred Biletnikoff deep down the middle, drawing the defense with him, and have Billy Cannon trail behind him by about five yards. Then Fred would tap the ball to Cannon."*

From News Dispatches of January 14:

Members of the Oakland Raiders, polled on the morning of the Super Bowl game, had the following observations:

Dan Conners, middle linebacker — "We camouflage our defenses a lot by moving in and out, listening to the audibles of quarterbacks and getting the rhythm down early. After a while, you can feel the cadence and get the tempo of the game. You have to have a feel for the timing. That presents a problem with Bart Starr. He is unrhythmic."

Kent McCloughan, corner back — "Boyd Dowler and Carroll Dale are bigger receivers than we're used to. I've never played against any that big. They are like tight ends, but with better speed. If our two outside defensive backs stop them, we have a chance."

Dan Birdwell, defensive tackle — "The Packers have been playing together for so long that they don't have to hold illegally. If one guy breaks down, another helps out. It's second nature to them."

Harry Schuh, offensive tackle — "Looking at films, Willie Davis is awful quick. He is strong on the pass. The game will have to be called real good by the officials in order to keep him honest."

Members of the Green Bay Packers, polled on the morning of the Super Bowl game, had the following observations:

Boyd Dowler, flanker — "I believe Oakland's defense may be a little better than Kansas City's was last year. Their corner backs are better."

Willie Wood, free safety — "The Oakland receivers rely on moves rather than speed. They don't make mistakes on their patterns. They don't have a Bob Hayes. But they don't have a Homer Jones, either."

Jerry Kramer, offensive right guard — "I got up this morning, put my undershorts on backwards and, for the first time in my life, I missed a team meeting. I was having breakfast with my wife when I suddenly realized that I was supposed to be someplace else. I guess I'm the only guy around here who's excited by this game."

THE OPENING MATCHUPS

GREEN BAY ON OFFENSE

No.	Player	Ht.	Wt.	Pos.
84	Carroll Dale	6-4	200	WR
86	Boyd Dowler	6-5	225	WR
81	Marv Fleming	6-4	235	TE
75	Forrest Gregg	6-4	250	RT
64	Jerry Kramer	6-3	245	RG
57	Ken Bowman	6-3	230	C
68	Gale Gillingham	6-3	255	LG
76	Bob Skoronski	6-3	250	LT
15	Bart Starr	6-1	200	QB
44	Donny Anderson	6-3	210	RB
36	Ben Wilson	6-2	225	FB

OAKLAND ON DEFENSE

No.	Player	Ht.	Wt.	Pos.
24	Willie Brown	6-1	205	RCB
47	Kent McCloughan	6-1	190	LCB
20	Warren Powers	6-0	190	SS
77	Ike Lassiter	6-5	270	LE
53	Dan Birdwell	6-4	250	LT
55	Dan Conners	6-1	230	MLB
74	Tom Keating	6-2	247	RT
83	Ben Davidson	6-7	275	RE
29	Howie Williams	6-1	190	FS
42	Bill Laskey	6-3	235	LLB
34	Gus Otto	6-2	220	RLB

OAKLAND ON OFFENSE

No.	Player	Ht.	Wt.	Pos.
89	Bill Miller	6-0	190	WR
25	Fred Biletnikoff	6-1	190	WR
33	Billy Cannon	6-1	215	TE
79	Harry Schuh	6-2	260	RT
65	Wayne Hawkins	6-0	240	RG
00	Jim Otto	6-2	248	C
63	Gene Upshaw	6-5	255	LG
76	Bob Svihus	6-4	245	LT
3	Daryle Lamonica	6-3	215	QB
40	Pete Banaszak	5-11	200	RB
35	Hewritt Dixon	6-1	230	FB

GREEN BAY ON DEFENSE

No.	Player	Ht.	Wt.	Pos.
21	Bob Jeter	6-1	205	RCB
26	Herb Adderley	6-0	210	LCB
40	Tom Brown	6-1	190	SS
87	Willie Davis	6-3	245	LE
77	Ron Kostelnik	6-4	260	LT
66	Ray Nitschke	6-3	240	MLB
74	Henry Jordan	6-3	250	RT
82	Lionel Aldridge	6-4	245	RE
24	Willie Wood	5-10	190	FS
89	Dave Robinson	6-3	240	LLB
60	Lee Roy Caffey	6-3	250	RLB

Jerry Kramer was so excited he couldn't put his underwear on right.

Chuck Mercein, fullback — "Anyone who gets a chance to play for the Packers is fortunate. But no one in his right mind could expect to have the good fortune I've had this season. I was especially delighted by the way the Packers accepted me as a member of the team . . . immediately."

Willie Davis, defensive end — "I guess this season will be remembered as the one in which we won when we had to. A 9–4–1 record isn't great, but nobody can say we didn't have it when we needed it."

Marv Fleming, tight end — "Our dressing room, after we win, is going to be quiet as usual. I can't imagine us throwing Lombardi into a shower or pouring champagne over his head."

MIAMI, Jan. 14 (UPI) — The Columbia Broadcasting System, which spent $2.5 million for television rights to today's Super Bowl game, is spending thousands of dollars more on equipment and personnel. The game will be covered by 12 cameras, including one in the Goodyear blimp. Four video-tape machines will be used for isolated replays and highlights. There will be slow motion in color and a stop-action disc recorder for replays. Ray Scott will handle the play-by-play, Pat Summerall will be the analyst, and Jack Kemp of the Buffalo Bills a special commentator. Frank Gifford and Jack Whitaker will do the postgame interviews in the dressing rooms.

A 30-foot-high Green Bay Packer advanced across the green carpet of the Orange Bowl just before the kickoff, snorting smoke from three-foot-wide nostrils. Facing him across the 50-yard line was a similar thirty-foot replica of an Oakland Raider. This was the symbolic beginning, more spectacular and less risky than the four thousand pigeons were last year. At any moment, it seemed the two figures would split open like Trojan horses and spew the respective teams onto the field in the most spectacular surprise since girls in G-strings started popping out of cakes.

From News Dispatches of January 14:

Starting lineups for the Super Bowl, announced just before game time, produced only one surprise. Packer coach Vince Lombardi is starting Ben Wilson at fullback instead of Chuck Mercein, who had started in the last two Green Bay victories over the Los Angeles Rams and the Dallas Cowboys. Green Bay won the toss and elected to receive. Temperature at kickoff was 68 degrees.

The Packers, with all the effervescence of overworked morticians, moved thirty-four yards in the middle of the field the first time they had the ball. Starr directed them from their own 34-yard line to the Oakland 32,

Don Chandler got Green Bay on the scoreboard first.

with Chandler kicking a thirty-nine-yard field goal for a 3–0 lead.

"I knew this would be my last game as a Packer," said Chandler. "I was through as a player in my own mind. Thankfully, this game was going to wrap up my best season in football. The year before, things were just the opposite. I knew I could go on kicking for a long time but I just didn't have it here — in my heart — for football anymore. It was time to get to know my kids, build up my business and plant some family roots."

Toward the end of the first quarter, Starr marched Green Bay on another of its long drives — consuming time and Oakland energy — from its own 3-yard line to the Oakland 13, and Chandler kicked another field goal for a 6–0 lead. The two big plays were a seventeen-yard pass to Carroll Dale, who got behind Willie Brown, and a fourteen-yard scramble by Starr himself.

The Oakland corner backs, Kent McCloughan and Willie Brown, playing much tighter on the Green Bay receivers than is customary in the NFL, were burned for a touchdown early in the second period when Starr, on first down from his own 38, connected with Dowler deep down the middle. Dowler ran the rest of the way unmolested. The play covered sixty-two yards and, with Chandler's point-after, gave Green Bay a 13–0 lead.

"I just bulled by McCloughan," said Dowler. "He was playing me tight and he bumped me and I ran through him. It was just a little post pattern, and when I got by him there was no one left to stop me."

The touchdown apparently aroused Oakland or at least put thoughts of being on the embarrassing side of a mismatch in the players' silver-coated heads. Lamonica, displaying some of the poise he admired so much in his counterpart, started sending Pete Banaszak and Hewritt Dixon into the middle of the Green Bay line and, for the first time, they started to make dents. Earlier, he was trying to send them wide, but Green Bay's linebackers came up fast and stopped them cold, indicating the speed of the Packer linebackers and the lack of it by Banaszak and Dixon. Now they were running right past Ron Kostelnik and Henry Jordan, behind the blocking of Gene Upshaw, Jim Otto and Wayne Hawkins.

With the ball on the Green Bay 23, Lamonica saw his split end, Bill Miller, slip behind the Packers' Tom Brown in the end zone and hit him with a pass for a touchdown. Blanda came in and kicked the extra point; Oakland had narrowed the Green Bay lead to 13–7.

"I was supposed to take Miller deep, but I played him too soft," said Brown. "Dave Robinson dropped back as far with him as he could and I should have taken him. But I didn't."

Just before the first half ended, Green Bay punted and Oakland's Rodger Bird called for a fair catch on his own 45-yard line. But he dropped the ball. Dick Capp, activated the day before the game, fell on it for Green Bay. With

Bill Miller scores on a pass from Daryle Lamonica.

seconds left on the clock, Starr tried two long pass plays and both failed. He finally threw one to Dowler for nine yards, giving Green Bay the ball on the Oakland 36. With six seconds left, Chandler kicked his third field goal, a forty-three-yarder, and Green Bay had a 16–7 half-time lead.

"At half time, Lombardi kept saying that nine points isn't enough," said Bengtson. "In the coaches' room, we went over the changes he wanted to make, but I guess they really weren't necessary the way it turned out. At the same time we were talking, a group of older players got together in a corner of the locker room — Gregg, Jordan, Nitschke, Davis, Starr, Dowler, Kramer, Skoronski, Thurston and McGee — and they vowed to play the last thirty minutes for the Old Man. They spread the word to the rest of the team and they told everybody to settle down, be cool and calculated in the second half, and we would win it easily."

Early in the third period, the Packers broke the game open on a play that, for them, was as patented as a power sweep. Starr, with third down and one on the Green Bay 40-yard line, faked to the fullback, Ben Wilson, going into the line, dropped back and passed to McGee, who had replaced Dowler. Starr, who had used the third-and-short-yardage pass many times in the NFL, caught the Raiders with their tight silver pants down.

McGee caught the ball behind Bird for a thirty-five-yard gain to the Oakland 25. "One of the safeties woke up late," said McGee. "He started over and Bart saw him and adjusted to throw away from him. That's why I had to turn around to catch the ball. Bart made a great throw."

Starr then threw short passes to Donny Anderson and Dale, moving the ball to the Oakland 2-yard line, from where Anderson scored. Chandler's extra point put the Packers ahead by 23–7. Chandler added his fourth field goal later in the third period from thirty-one yards out. It hit the crossbar and then went over it.

Early in the fourth period, Herb Adderley, Green Bay's left corner back, intercepted a pass by Lamonica and, with help from blocks by Jordan (at the 10) and Kostelnik (at the 5), ran it back sixty yards for a touchdown. Chandler's kick made it 33–7 and gave him fifteen points for the day — one more than the entire Oakland team would score. "We designed the defense to take away their runs," said Adderley. "We wanted to make them put the ball in the air. This time, Lamonica was trying to hit Biletnikoff on a slant-in, and I played the ball and cut in front of him. It was no gamble."

All that remained at this point was the continued blinking of the white-on-green clock. Oakland added its final touchdown later in the fourth quarter, and it was so insignificant it could not be described as even anti-climactic. Lamonica hit Miller with another twenty-three-yard pass, with Miller getting behind Brown again — just as he had in the second period.

Herb Adderley takes a pass away from Fred Biletnikoff.

Donny Anderson leaps into the end zone for a Packer tally.

Blanda's extra point completed the scoring at 33–14, Green Bay.

"Right after the final gun, Jerry Kramer and Forrest Gregg picked up Lombardi," said Bengtson, "and they said to him, 'One more time, coach.' Lombardi looked down at them and said, 'This is the best way to leave a football field.' "

As newsmen assembled in the Green Bay locker room, Max McGee told them that he was retiring as a Packer.

"This was my last game," McGee, thirty-five, said. "I really didn't expect to play in it at all. I was kidding Dowler before the game, telling him to get hurt so I could catch one more pass. Damned if he didn't. Damned if I didn't."

"I thought I was ready for this one," said Gregg, thirty-four, completing his eleventh Packer season and his eighth championship game. "But when I got out there, I just didn't have the zip. I didn't have the zip I had against Dallas two weeks ago, or against Los Angeles the week before that. Today it was mechanical. I was like a robot. It's been a helluva long season."

"It's tough to get up when you've been on the stick for two big games," said Lee Roy Caffey. "I know we did not play as well as we have in the past. We made mistakes we don't make in most games. But, oh shit, it turned out all right for us, didn't it?"

"The AFL is getting better," said Henry Jordan. "If they improve as much each year, they'll be on a par with us soon. I think this was a tougher team than Kansas City, especially on defense. The AFL is becoming more sophisticated on offense. I think the league has always had good personnel, but the blocks were more subtle and conceived better this year.

"They're in the same position we were in before our first championship game against Philadelphia. That was the first big one for a lot of us. We thought we were ready and would win. We weren't and we didn't. All of us have regretted that ever since. We have never forgotten it. We don't talk much about it, but it's always in the back of our heads before a game like this. I don't think Oakland will forget this one either."

"It wasn't our best effort," said Lombardi. "All year it seemed like as soon as we got a couple touchdowns ahead, we would let up. Maybe that's the sign of a veteran team. I don't know."

"You're always disappointed when you lose. It's tough in life to accept

Vince Lombardi went out as a winner.

defeat and we're not used to it. We made mistakes, like a breakdown in pass coverage that gave Boyd Dowler a touchdown, and that fumble that gave them a field goal at the end of the first half. But that's why people win and lose," said John Rauch, ending the week in the Oakland locker room with the same hyperbole with which he began it.

Up in the press box, writers were voting for Bart Starr as the game's Most Valuable Player, a distinction that would earn for him, courtesy of *Sport* magazine, a new Corvette. But, as a reward for pure artistry in the pits, there were observers who felt that Tom Keating of Oakland and Gale Gillingham of Green Bay were deserving of something, perhaps a turbo-charged ambulance each. Like whistling trash collectors who never drop a morsel, they performed their jobs impeccably.

Jerry Izenberg described it in the Newark Star-Ledger:

Still, Oakland was not without a hero. His name was Tom Keating, and he played this game on one leg. He fought a brutally intense war with the Packers' Gale Gillingham. In pride and guts . . . in simple basic arithmetic . . . this was really the only genuine Super Bowl played in Miami yesterday.

Keating, a defensive tackle, came into this game with a right ankle the size of a herniated softball. He was not supposed to play at all. As for Mr. Gillingham, well, Mr. Gillingham is relatively new in this league and back when Mr. Keating was healthy, the Oaklands privately thought he would eat Mr. Gillingham in no more time than six large bites.

Yesterday, they went at it for 60 minutes. The Packers' superb balance made everything else around them degenerate. But like two coal-stokers, fighting for the championship of the Pacific Tuna Fleet, they brought out the best in each other long after the rest of the game had become a laugher.

Play after play, Gillingham would rise up from his left guard spot and put his body into Tom Keating's. An over-sized elbow-bandage on Gillingham's arm turned crimson. Blood spattered his white jersey. Fatigue seeped across his battered face.

Play after play, Gillingham did not look for Keating because Keating was always in front of him or at least halfway through his stomach. Keating's ankle went from softball to basketball in the first quarter. Blood ran down his left arm from a gash.

Sequence after sequence, Keating would stagger off the field and Gillingham would sigh a little. But damned if he wouldn't be right back again, dragging his big round ankle behind him.

This was the real Super Bowl and no two ever played it better.

GREEN BAY, Jan. 15 (AP) — *An overflow crowd stormed Austin-Straubel Airport in sub-freezing weather last night to welcome home members of the Green Bay Packers football team, Super Bowl champions for the second straight year.*

NFL Commissioner Pete Rozelle congratulates Lombardi.

Despite the Green Bay exuberance, there was little to justify the wasting of three hours to watch this Super Bowl game either in person or in front of television picture tubes (could this have been what Mencken envisioned as "boobus Americanus"?). Like the year before, it was a matchup of a good football team and a condescending one. It was questionable whether the American Football League would ever win one of these games. The Raiders, like the Chiefs before them, were not disgraced; on the other hand, neither were they overly combative. For two straight years, the Packers merely showed up and took the title home with them, like guilty bullies stealing Halloween candy from underprotected paper bags. The letdown was especially evident in the press box, where close games usually become classics and mediocre ones interesting, at least. But fandangoing through the curtain of TassIzvestia rhetoric, Jerry Izenberg and Robert Lipsyte of *The New York Times* put Super Bowl II in its printed perspective.

Izenberg:

Softly, with all the taste and subtlety of the Bombay bread riots, Greater Miami and the Orange Bowl Stadium stretched their arms forth to nestle the second annual Super Bowl game to their bosoms.

They started nuzzling at 2:45 p.m., with 140 yards worth of sousaphones, cornets and French horns. They finished nuzzling at 6 p.m., by sidearming a barrage of toilet paper from the upper stands.

Somehow, in between, the Green Bay Packers and the Oakland Raiders managed to get the Super Bowl played. The Green Bays won it, 33–14. The Green Bays also won it, 35–10, last year. The American League, therefore, over a span of two seasons, has cut the margin by six points. At their current rate of progress, the Americans should manage to get a tie somewhere around 1971.

Lipsyte:

It was an anticlimactic game in the sense that the millions spent to televise the game, the thousands to promote it, and the enormous emotion and work spent preparing for it, were not rewarded by either sustained drama or even moments of great excitement. Days before, an Oakland Raider said that playing the Packers would be like "playing our fathers." The boys of the Golden West were not quite ready yet.

"A week or so after the game, Vince and I got together in his office overlooking Highland Avenue in downtown Green Bay," said Phil Bengtson. "He told me then of his plans — he was going to step down and be the full-time general manager, and he wanted me to succeed him as head coach. Would I accept? 'Yes,' I told him. 'Yes, I will accept. It doesn't exactly come as a surprise.'

"Vince got up from behind his desk and walked over to the window and watched the slow line of traffic for a while. 'You know, Phil,' he finally said, 'I marvel that I tried to do both jobs for all these years.' He walked back to his desk, sat down again and said, 'You know, everybody is going to be second-guessing us. We're both taking a pretty big leap. But I think we're both doing what we feel we have to do. The sporting end of football is almost all emotion. The business end has to be hard practicality. Right?' I nodded in agreement and, before I left his office, he told me he would prepare a news release to announce the changeover, for delivery at a sports dinner on February 1 at the Oneida Golf and Riding Club.

"The day of the announcement, Vince's receptionist, Sarah McLain, came into my office and sat down. 'I've never seen him so nervous,' she said. 'The door has been closed for more than an hour with the telephone off the hook.' Vince was working on his statement. The rest of his staff, meanwhile, was making last-minute preparations to accommodate more than a hundred sportsmen and newswriters who were going to attend what had been planned as an intimate dinner for a select few. The whole scene was getting as tense as the kickoff of a championship game.

"At the dinner that night, the moment for the announcement finally came and, as Vince stepped up to the battery of microphones, his hands were trembling. He pulled five sheets of paper from his breast pocket and spread them on the speaker's lectern. He had handwritten his remarks in huge script letters three-quarters of an inch tall with a grease pen just like the ones he used to sketch play patterns on a notepad. He looked around the crowded room, raised a closed fist to his mouth and forced a slight smile.

"'What I have to say is not completely without emotion,' he began. 'Because of the emotion involved, I felt I could not trust myself to say what I must say unless it was written.' He outlined very briefly the growth of pro football and the Packers, and the increasing responsibility of the general manager's job. By now the audience was starting to squirm in anticipation.

"'I believe it is impractical for me to do both jobs, and feel that I must relinquish one of them. . . .' A moment later he read the last words on his paper: 'Gentlemen, let me introduce you to the new head coach of the Packers. . . .' When he spoke my name, I rose, and he led the applause for me. There were tears in his eyes and, as I stood there, I felt more drained of energy than after the toughest game I could remember. When you make your living telling other men to maintain their poise while performing near-impossible tasks, it's strange to suddenly find yourself thrust into the same situation. But somehow, we made it.

"The torch had passed."

"There were some people around who were saying that Vince had copped out on us," said Donny Anderson. "But that wasn't the case at all. I was finishing my rookie season with the Packers and people were saying that

67

Jim Grabowski and Travis Williams and Gale Gillingham and myself represented the future of the team, and that if we were going to develop properly there was only one man around who could oversee the job — and that was Vince. I didn't feel any resentment toward Vince for stepping down as coach, and I don't think any of the other young Packers did either. It was more a feeling of deep depression, gnawing on the inside. I know I asked myself many times, 'The greatest coach you ever played for is through, and where do you go from here?' But after a while I snapped out of it and realized that Vince made a smart move for himself. He had no place to go but down with the Packers. Besides, he had his own life to live, and how could we begrudge him anything?

"I first got the news that Vince had retired as coach the morning after the banquet in Green Bay. A friend called me in Dallas from Milwaukee. Then I turned on the radio to make positively sure. But I wasn't surprised. The way Vince had looked at each of us during the week before the Super Bowl game was a giveaway. He would look at us like a father looks at a son he is about to push into the world on his own two feet. It was like he was remembering things about each of us and evaluating each of us in his own mind for the last time. It was sad, almost heartbreaking, and the whole team was a little depressed. I'm sure it contributed to our rather uninspired performance in the game.

"But once the game was over and I adjusted to the fact that Vince would no longer be coaching the Packers, I forgot all about it and tried to wipe the slate clean. Vince was an offensive coach and his successor, Phil Bengtson, was a defensive coach. That left me and the rest of the backs in funny positions. I was wondering what it would be like to play for a defense-oriented coach? Would he know the little tricks on offense? Would he treat the backs with the same affection that Vince did? Would the day ever come when we wished we had Vince back with us? But other than that, Vince's retirement caused no catastrophe among the young players. Those who liked Vince were sad; those who didn't were happy.

"After the Super Bowl and his retirement, I didn't see Vince personally for quite a while. I wondered a lot what it would be like without him, but I never held his retirement against him. Some people were saying that Vince was contradicting his own principles by stepping down. They said he quit because the team was getting old, and that he dumped a lot of has-beens into Bengtson's lap. They were going around asking, 'Where is Vince's dedication now? Where is his loyalty to the Packers? Where are the sacrifice, the unity and the discipline he preached?' I laughed at all of them, because they didn't know what they were talking about.

"Anybody who had been around Vince knew that he made the only move he could possibly have made at the time."

69

Donny Anderson looked toward the future.

SUPER BOWL III

"I GUARANTEE IT"

Participants — New York Jets, champions of the American Football League, and Baltimore Colts, champions of the National Football League.

Date — January 12, 1969.

Site — Orange Bowl Stadium, Miami, Florida.

Time — 3:05 P.M., EST.

Attendance — 75,377.

Radio and Television — National Broadcasting Company (TV and Radio).

Regular-Season Records — New York, 11-3; Baltimore, 13-1.

Playoff Records — New York defeated Oakland Raiders, 27-23, for AFL title; Baltimore defeated Cleveland Browns, 34-0, for NFL title.

Players' Shares — $15,000 to each member of winning team; $7,500 to each member of losing team.

Gate Receipts — Estimated $750,000.

Radio-TV Receipts — $2,500,000.

Officials — Referee, Tommy Bell, NFL; Umpire, Walt Parker, AFL; Linesman, George Murphy, NFL; Back Judge, Jack Reader, AFL; Field Judge, Joe Gonzales, NFL; Line Judge, Cal Lepore, AFL.

Coaches — Weeb Ewbank, New York; Don Shula, Baltimore.

SANTA BARBARA, Calif., Jan. 2 (AP) — Jimmy (The Greek) Snyder, Las Vegas odds-maker who sets the nation's betting line on everything from Triple Crown races to Presidential ones, was admitted into the University of California at Santa Barbara Hospital today for treatment of acute abdominal pains. Before he checked in, however, he listed the Baltimore Colts as 18-point favorites to defeat the New York Jets in the Super Bowl.

NEW YORK, Jan. 2 (NEA) — The New York Jets will beat the Baltimore Colts in the Super Bowl. Some reasons are: The transiting Jupiter is sextile the natal Mars and Pluto is trine the midheaven and — well, there are eight other favorable points. Greek? No, astrology, pure and celestial. Snuff-sniffing, bearded professional astrologer Jonathan Booth drew up horoscopes for the Jets and Colts to determine the winner of their game Jan. 12. Booth finds, in capsule form, that the Pisces Jets will have a great desire to win, while the Aquarius Colts will be plagued by overconfidence. Booth, who has never seen a football game in his life, did not predict a final score. But he said: "The Jets have 10 aspects going for them, the Colts only six. That could be it."

Late on the afternoon of January 3, the New York Jets were assembling in the VIP Lounge of the Northeast Airlines Terminal at Kennedy International Airport in Long Island. They would be flying to Fort Lauderdale at six o'clock on this Thursday night in a yellow Boeing 727 to start training for Super Bowl III against the Baltimore Colts.

The topic of conversation among early arrivals was, of course, Joe Namath. The Jets' quarterback had surprised even his own teammates when he committed the cardinal sin in sports a few days earlier — evaluating an opponent in less than flattering terms for public consumption. He said that Earl Morrall, who would be quarterbacking the Colts in the Super Bowl, was not as good as many of the quarterbacks in the American Football League, and he rated Daryle Lamonica of Oakland, John Hadl of San Diego, Bob Griese of Miami, Babe Parilli, his own replacement, and himself as being clearly superior. If there is one virtue American sports fans — cigar butts of men, Norman Mailer called them — demand from their prototyped athletes, it is humility; the sacrifice, however superficial it may be, of one's individuality for the alleged betterment of the team, league, sport and, ultimately, the society. But Joe Namath was as prototypic a football player as Muhammad Ali was a heavyweight boxing champion.

For years, sports pages had been filled with a montage of Namathania, Beaver Falls Alabama Bear Bryant Drinking Suspension Orange Bowl $400,000 Sonny Werblin Night Clubs Broads Llama Rugs Johnnie Walker Red Knee OperationsWhiteShoes12RookieofYearPlayerofYearFuManchu$10,000Shave ad infinitum. He and Ali emerged from the stereotyped rubble of the mid-1960's to challenge the roles traditional sports fans had designated for their athletes. Whereas Ali, after becoming heavyweight champion, was the first black athlete to publicly proclaim himself militant about something other than left jabs, right crosses and paychecks, Namath was the first white athlete to rise above the long-standing hallucination that public humility was the appropriate repayment for the opportunity to succeed in sports. As Ali reveled in his blackness, Namath reveled in his self-indulgence and, in both cases, they became the very best at what they did in sports while employing arrogant façades that challenged further a public they had sub-consciously damned.

Both had negative appeal to the audiences in Middle America's theaters, the sports stadiums from Boston to San Diego. Millions of dollars had been spent in the hope — indeed, the anticipated delight — of seeing Ali and Namath receive their first tastes of public humility at the hands of the more regimented ErnieTerrellsFloydPattersonsZoraFolleysRonMcDolesIke LassitersSteveDeLongs, all prospective, but unsuccessful, administrators of lashes at the whipping post. If America's traditional sports followers were ever going to press Ali and Namath to their contourless bosoms, the prerequisite was going to be public groveling by both in some moist dirt.

But Namath, wearing low-cut white shoes in a sea of high-topped black-on-green, the catalytic figure in every game he ever played as a pro, and Ali, wearing white shoes and manipulating the emotions of anyone who ever watched him fight, looked tradition in its overbearing eye and then poked a finger into it. Many times, both said that athletic images were frauds. Why, said Ali, can't a black athlete be proud of his blackness, and why can't he be called what he wishes? Why, said Namath, can't an athlete admit publicly to drinking alcohol, smoking tobacco, making love to beautiful women — if, indeed, he does? Traditionalists answered them by removing them from the mainstream and by clouding their accomplishments in controversy. Much of America, it seemed, wanted its athletes dished up on celibate platters, with no side orders of humanity.

When Ali joined the Fruit of Islam, commonly known as the Black Muslim sect, and changed his name to Muhammad Ali, forever abandoning Cassius Marcellus Clay, boxing fans refused to call him by his new name lest they condescendingly recognize the Muslims, at the time the most threatening of all black groups. But the same people for years had been calling Joseph L. Barrow *Joe Louis,* Arnold Raymond Cream *Jersey Joe Walcott,* Giuseppe Antonio Berardinelli *Joey Maxim,* Anthony Florian Zaleski *Tony Zale* and Walker Smith *Sugar Ray Robinson.* Joe Namath got into the name-changing act while at Alabama, facetiously adding a Willie to his first name — a political gesture that endeared him to the Billy Rays and the Jimmy Johns, Southern-borns who were his teammates at the time, and hoodwinked an entire generation into calling him "Joe Willie." But up in Beaver Falls, Pennsylvania, the yellowed birth records at Providence Hospital on Fourth Avenue show that on Memorial Day, 1943, the third son of Rose and John Namath was properly christened Joseph Alexander.

After the Jets beat Oakland in the AFL championship game, Jimmy Breslin wrote a magazine story that said that Namath had spent the night before the game ensconced in his apartment with a luscious young lady, alternating between her and the white leather bar. The next morning, the story said, he bade her farewell with a pat on her delectable rump, put on his mink coat and went off to Shea Stadium to become the outstanding player in the game. When asked about the article, Namath said it was true — except for two things: "The bar isn't white and I wasn't wearing my mink."

As he sat in his usual airplane seat — second row, coach, left side of the aisle — waiting for takeoff to Fort Lauderdale, Namath was approached by Dave Anderson of *The New York Times.*

"Still feel that way about Morrall?" Anderson asked.

"Yes," said Namath. "I said it and I mean it. Anybody who knows football players knows Lamonica throws better than Morrall. I watch all quarterbacks, and I study what they do. I read today where some NFL guy joked about Lamonica and me throwing nearly a hundred passes last Sunday. We threw ninety-seven, but what's so bad about that? How many

Baltimore's Earl Morrall was an MVP, but Joe Namath put the rap on him.

NFL teams have quarterbacks who complete as many passes as we do? In our league, we throw a lot more to our wide receivers than they do in theirs. I completed forty-nine percent of my passes this season, but I could've completed eighty percent if I dumped the ball off to my backs like they do in theirs.

"You put Babe Parilli with Baltimore instead of Morrall and Baltimore might be better. Babe throws better than Morrall. Listen, I don't have anything against Morrall, personally, it's just that I don't think he's that good a quarterback. That's my opinion. I'm entitled to it, right?

"If the Colts need newspaper clippings to get up for a game, then they're in a helluva lot of trouble."

In Baltimore, Earl Morrall was asked about Joe Namath's evaluation of him by a reporter. Morrall, his crew-cut straight and tall, as if an irate carpenter had pounded a week's worth of nails flawlessly into his skull, did not dodge the question.

"Joe is getting his newspaper space," he said, "and that's what he's after, isn't it? He seems to thrive on being in the limelight. He's a guy who relishes publicity. Look, any player on any team has information and opinions on other players that would send newspapermen running to their typewriters and command a great deal of newspaper space the next day. But players keep these opinions to themselves — at least that's the way it's been traditionally. Maybe Namath represents the new breed of athlete, the kind of athlete the coming generation wants. I hope not.

"When you've been playing football for twelve years, as I have been, you eventually come up against virtually every type of individual, from the quiet introvert to the swinger and loudmouth. Some guys never get their names in anything but the game programs. Other guys would do anything, or say anything, to get their names in the paper.

"Neither characteristic, as far as I'm concerned, has any effect on what happens on the football field."

> *FORT LAUDERDALE, Jan. 3 (AP) — The New York Jets, champions of the American Football League, arrived here today to begin training for the Super Bowl game. They will be using the same facilities the Green Bay Packers used last year — the Gault Ocean Mile Motel for lodging, and Fort Lauderdale Stadium for practice sessions.*

From News Dispatches of January 3:

The first two visitors the New York Jets had today after settling into their quarters at the Gault Ocean Mile Motel were members of the Federal

Bureau of Investigation. The FBI agents said they were making a routine investigation of Joe Namath's room.

"There was a threat on the guy's life a few weeks ago in New York," said one of the agents. "We think the guy who made it is in the Miami area now. We talked to Namath for a while, checked the room out, then left. The room is in a good spot. His balcony faces the beach, not the pool, like the others do. If somebody is going to take a shot at him, he won't be able to hide in the palm trees around the pool. He's got to stand out there on the beach, to get a look at him. If he does that, he'll never get away."

The room, numbered 534, was described by the hotel as the Governor's Suite. A year ago, it was occupied by Vince Lombardi, coach of the Green Bay Packers.

Wilbur Charles (Weeb) Ewbank, coach of the Jets who had coached Baltimore to an NFL title in 1959 and was fired by the Colts four years later, walked into the lobby of the Gault Ocean Mile limping and carrying a gray cane.

"What's wrong?" he was asked.

"Remember when the players carried me off the field after the Oakland game?" he said. "Well, some kid came along and swung on my right leg halfway to the locker room. It really irritated the hip joint.

"The writers said that after I got to the locker room tears of joy were rolling down my cheeks. They were tears, period."

> *FORT LAUDERDALE, Jan. 4 (AP) — Jim Hudson, safetyman for the New York Jets, joined the team today after arriving here on a commercial flight. He had been given an extra day off to take his wife and son back home to Austin, Texas.*

"Damn airlines," said Hudson, slumped in front of his locker at Fort Lauderdale Stadium. "Been on damn airplanes for two days. I took my wife and little boy to Newark two days ago to fly to Dallas. We had so much junk, closing out our New York apartment, I had to hire a truck. We missed the plane at Newark and had to wait three hours for the next one. When we got to Dallas, we had to wait four hours for the flight to Austin. By the time we got home it was three o'clock in the morning. I got a couple hours of sleep, then got up to come here yesterday. But when I got to Dallas my flight to Miami was canceled. Weather, or somethin'. I had to wait five hours for one to New Orleans, then I waited another hour in New Orleans to go to Atlanta, and when I got to Atlanta there were no more flights to Fort Lauderdale. But they had one that stopped in Jacksonville and Tampa going to Miami, so I took it. When I got to Miami, I jumped a limousine. I got to

the hotel at five o'clock this morning.

"To make it worse, the damn airlines lost my baggage. No idea at all where it is. All I got is the suit I was wearing."

Knowing that he was Joe Namath's roommate, a reporter asked Hudson if he would borrow some of Joe's clothes — "They fit you, don't they?"

"Yeah, if I get desperate," said Hudson.

> *FORT LAUDERDALE, Jan. 5 (UPI) — A crowd of 250 people was on hand today at Fort Lauderdale International Airport to greet the Baltimore Colts, champions of the National Football League, who arrived by charter jet to begin training for the Super Bowl game against the New York Jets. The Colts will be quartered at the Statler-Hilton Hotel and use the facilities of St. Andrew's Boys School in Boca Raton for practice sessions.*

Don Shula, coach of the Colts, who once played for Weeb Ewbank and later succeeded him, talked briefly with the press en route from the airplane to the charter bus that was waiting to take the team to its hotel. Yes, Shula said, it was cold in Baltimore. No, he said, the frozen ground had not hampered his team's practices; in fact, the club had practiced quite well. No, he said, his practices at Boca Raton would not be open to the public; the Jets could send a spy to hide among the spectators. As he walked toward the bus, Bill Johns of the Statler-Hilton Hotel walked over to Shula and stopped him.

"Don," he said, "I've got a limousine waiting to take you to the hotel."

"No, thanks," said Shula. "I always ride with my players."

After checking into the hotel, some of the Colts wandered aimlessly in the lobby or went into the Don Quixote Room for dinner. One of them was Lou Michaels, the place-kicker, whose older brother, Walt, was defensive coach of the Jets. Years earlier, when they were playing for different teams, they had been accused of trading secrets.

"I'm not going to talk to Walt until after the game," said Lou Michaels, "if he still wants to talk then. If I know my brother like I think I know him, he's not going to be talking to me either."

The telephone in Johnny Sample's room rang at the Gault Motel. He had been expecting a call as soon as the Colts arrived — from Lenny Lyles, a close friend and his roommate in 1958 when they played for Baltimore. In the Super Bowl, they would be rival corner backs, an unusual situation for two men who had taken their families vacationing together several times in the past.

Coach Weeb Ewbank had led both the Colts and the Jets to championships.

Sample picked up the phone, and it was Lyles.

"John," said the familiar voice, "the champions of the National Football League have arrived."

The Colts became champions of the National Football League by defeating the Cleveland Browns, 34–0, on a gray, misty Sunday afternoon before 84,000 people in Cleveland's Municipal Stadium. They held Leroy Kelly of the Browns, the NFL's leading rusher, to twenty-seven yards.

Before the start of the Colts-Browns game, two hundred people had gathered in the Wigwam Club, high in the rafters of the stadium and overlooking Lakeside Avenue and downtown Cleveland, to watch the start of the Jets-Oakland game for the AFL championship. Two color television sets were installed for the occasion, as the AFL game in New York was to start an hour earlier than the game in Cleveland. As Namath and Daryle Lamonica of Oakland started throwing passes deep to their wide receivers early in the game, the NFL partisans grimaced in contempt.

"What you are watching," said Harry McClelland of the Cleveland *Press*, "is known as Mickey Mouse football."

As the Jets filed out of Fort Lauderdale Stadium after their Saturday practice, Winston Hill, the Jets' offensive left tackle, lingered in front of a mirror, brushing his hair. A sportswriter approached and asked him what he remembered about being a Colt in training camp in 1963. The sportswriter asked if he was bitter about being cut.

"I don't think about such things," said Hill. "Every few years I go back over my life and cross out everything that's unpleasant."

George Sauer, Jr., the split end, came up behind him and rested his chin on Hill's left shoulder. "Why, then," said Sauer, "don't you cross out your face?"

On Sunday morning, January 5, Mark Smolinski, captain of the Jets' special teams, went to nine-thirty Mass at St. Pius X Church in Fort Lauderdale. Sitting a few pews in front of him was Don Shula, the Colts' coach, whom Smolinski quickly recognized. Just before the Mass ended, Smolinski walked out into the rain, assuring that there would be no accidental meeting between him and Shula. Like Winston Hill, he had been cut by Shula in 1963.

"I don't have any hard feelings toward the guy," said Smolinski, "it's just that I didn't want to have to say hello to him."

Later, as the Jets assembled at the stadium, Joe Namath walked into the locker room, his face and eyes glazed over. He started getting dressed

81

Baltimore's Don Shula had played for Ewbank, and succeeded him as coach.

and was singing to himself:

"V-I-C-T-O-R-Y, Are We In? Well, I Guess. Beaver Falls High School—yes, yes, yes. . . . V-I-C-T-O-R-Y, Are We In? Well, I Guess. Beaver Falls High School — yes, yes, yes. . . ."

Out in Boca Raton, Earl Morrall, who had just been voted by players in the NFL as the winner of the Jim Thorpe Trophy — their Most Valuable Player award — was talking to reporters about the Colts' game plan.

"Preparing for this game is no different from preparing for any other," Morrall said. "There is no such thing as a completely 'new' opponent. Every team we play is 'new' to some degree. In every game, we face players or playing situations that we've never faced before. The challenge is in adjusting to them, immediately, before any damage is done. I'd say we're preparing for the Jets the same way we prepared for the Browns or the Redskins or the Dallas Cowboys.

"We're going over six or seven Jet game films and doing the usual analyzing — charting the frequency with which they use each of their offensive and defensive formations, things like that. Ed Rutledge, one of our assistant coaches, scouted the Jets last week against Oakland. He took notes on both clubs and watched especially for injuries. Rutledge is a great student of pregame warm-ups. He said they always give a clue or two as to which players are in shape and which ones are hurting.

"As for Namath, I've only seen him play on television, three or four times. He has a fast release and sets up quickly. He backpedals a lot deeper than most quarterbacks in our league, but I guess he wants to protect his knees. He doesn't do any scrambling, but he doesn't get thrown for losses too much either. I attribute that to his quick release more than anything else.

"I don't think we're complacent or overconfident. What are we, eighteen-point favorites? That puts the pressure on us to win big. A close victory by us would be a moral victory for them."

That night, Lou Michaels, the Colts' place-kicker, and Dan Sullivan, a guard, stopped in Jimmy Fazio's Restaurant in Fort Lauderdale for dinner. After finishing their meal, they went to the bar. Spotting Namath and Jim Hudson of the Jets standing in a corner, Michaels left Sullivan and walked over to them.

"Namath," he said, "Lou Michaels."

Namath nodded.

"You're doing a lot of talking, boy," Michaels said.

"There's a lot to talk about," said Namath. "We're going to kick hell out of your team."

"Haven't you ever heard of the word 'modesty'?" Michaels asked.

Namath didn't answer. Hudson nudged him to a table and they sat down and ordered dinner. Before the food came, Michaels and Sullivan pulled up chairs and sat down with them.

"You still here?" Namath said to Michaels.

"Damn right I'm still here," Michaels said. "I want to hear everything you've got to say."

"I'm going to pick you apart."

"You're going to find it hard throwing out of a well."

"My blockers will give me time."

"I never heard Johnny Unitas or Bobby Layne talk like that."

"I believe that."

"Even if we do get in trouble, we'll send in Unitas, the master."

"I hope you do, because that'll mean the game is too far gone."

"Too far what . . . ?"

Namath excused himself and walked over to a nearby table to say hello to some friends. Hudson, meanwhile, attempted to calm Michaels.

"Don't pay any attention to what Joe said," said Hudson. "You've got to understand him."

Michaels grumbled something about cocky kids and ordered another drink. But Namath returned before the drink arrived.

"Suppose we kick hell out of you," said Michaels. "Just suppose we do that? Then what'll you do, Namath?"

"I'll tell you what I'll do," said Namath. "I'll sit down right in the middle of the field and I'll cry."

Michaels had become Richard Nixon debating John Kennedy; he reluctantly backed down and changed the subject, like a poker player holding two threes and raising might do after having his bluff called. Slowly, a tense truce settled over the table. When the check came, Namath paid it with a hundred-dollar bill.

"You guys got a ride back to the hotel?" Namath asked.

"No," said Michaels, "but we'll take a cab."

"Don't be silly," said Namath, "we'll drop you."

Together, the four players left. After departing from Namath's car in the driveway of the Statler-Hilton, Michaels turned to Sullivan and said, "You know, he's not such a bad kid after all."

But the next day, stories of a Namath-Michaels confrontation were on the wires and appearing in newspapers across the country. Some reports described it as a near fistfight. Others a heated debate. Still others, a typical meeting of both sides of the generation gap. But there were members of the Baltimore Colts who were hardly impressed with Lou Michaels' performance. Stopping him in the Statler-Hilton lobby the next morning, one of them said, "We heard about it, Lou."

"Heard about what?"

"About how Namath bought you off with a hundred-dollar bill."

"He's a good guy . . . a good guy."

"Then how come you were ready to bust him one in the mouth?"

"It wasn't like that at all. . . ."

Later, another Colt said, "Joe Namath is the 837th guy that Lou Michaels has challenged. But if Lou had belted him, he would have been about the thirty-seventh guy that Lou actually hit."

Said Hudson, Namath's companion, "What else can you expect when two hard-headed coalminers from Pennsylvania get together?"

From the New York Jets' Itinerary:

"Monday, January 6, will be Picture Day. All players will be at Fort Lauderdale Stadium at 10 A.M. White game uniforms will be worn."

Several dozen newspaper photographers and television crews had assembled at the practice fields to shoot all the pregame footage they would need. This would be the only time they would be allowed to take pictures of the Jets' and Colts' players in uniform before the game.

Football players, many sportswriters agree, are the most cooperative of all athletes, except for boxers, in the area of press relations. But on this day the New York Jets would shatter the myth completely. Four of their best players — Namath, Hudson, Matt Snell and Emerson Boozer — did not show up. Namath and Hudson said that they wanted to take advantage of the day off; Snell and Boozer said that they had been sleeping. Frank Ramos, the Jets' public relations director, was embarrassed and pressed Boozer on the issue. Ramos said a call had been put through to Snell and Boozer's room and there was no answer.

"We heard it ringing," said Boozer, "and we ignored it. We thought it was just another silly call."

At noon, in the Don Quixote Room of the Statler-Hilton, Don Shula was preparing to hold a press conference. Before the formal program started, a writer told him that Namath hadn't shown up for Picture Day.

"Namath what?" said Shula. "He didn't show up for Photo Day? What the hell is Weeb doing?"

When the questioning started, the topic, of course, was Namath. Shula responded to the questions with stock answers, as if he were pressing imaginary buttons in his mind signaling the appropriate IBM cards filed away in his brain to come descending down the chute: Yes, Namath has quick release. Yes, his downfield vision is good. Yes, he backpedals more than NFL quarterbacks do. Yes, he'll unload the ball. Yes, he has fast feet.

Matt Snell was one of four Jets who were camera-shy before the Super Bowl

Yeshisarmisstrong,yeshispassesareaccurateyesyesyesyes.

"But," Shula concluded, "Namath hasn't been throwing against the defenses that Earl has been throwing against."

When he mentioned Morrall, a new line of Namath questioning began. The first questioner asked Shula for his reaction to Namath's criticism of Morrall.

"I don't know how Namath can rap Earl," he answered. "After all, Earl is No. 1 in the NFL. He's thrown all those touchdown passes. He's thrown for a great percentage without using dinky flare passes. He's the Player of the Year. He's had a great season for us and we're proud of him. Anyone who doesn't give him the credit he deserves is wrong. . . ."

Shula's voice rose and the veins in his neck thickened.

"But I guess Namath can say whatever the hell he wants."

From News Dispatches of January 6:

Weeb Ewbank, coach of the Jets, received a letter today that read: "Dear Weeb . . . Attached are three plays drawn for what I call the 'Flying I' formation. The formation can be shifted into or shifted out of as you see it. The main idea is the confusion factor. Baltimore has never seen your team run or pass from this formation. If you can use it, we can discuss terms later. It's no crazier than the other plays and formations you probably get."

Ewbank, when asked if he would implement the formation, said: "Hell, no. It'd confuse the Colts, but it would confuse us worse."

Earl Morrall, after returning from the Colts' photo session, was asked by his wife, Jane, why their room in the Statler-Hilton was cluttered by crumbs from cheese crackers.

"You don't usually eat those things," she said to him.

"I know," said Morrall, "but I've been too busy to eat lunch. Too many writers around wanting to talk to me."

"That's the price you pay for fame."

"I'll pay it," said Morrall. "I'll pay it."

While Matt Snell, Verlon Biggs, Jeff Richardson, Winston Hill, John Dockery and Mike Stromberg were on chartered fishing boats three miles off the coast of Fort Lauderdale, enjoying the Jets' day off, the game plan was being completed by Ewbank and his staff. It would be mimeographed and fastened inside folders, like a doctoral thesis. Each of the coaches and the quarterbacks would receive typewritten instructions, and Betty Spencer, wife of the offensive coach, had volunteered to do the typing.

"It's two pages long," she said. "I thought it would only be one."

"They usually are," her husband said. "But this is a big game."

The Jets' game plan, essentially, looked like this:

Page 1 — A list of players on the Colts' defensive teams, their names and their numbers.

Page 2 — A list of plays the Jet coaches felt would work best against the Baltimore defense. Also the three basic offensive formations from which the Jets would operate — the flank, split and slot. From these formations, the Jets could run a combination of forty-six different plays.

Page 3 — Diagrams of the Colts' six primary defenses.

Page 4 — Diagrams of the Colts' four stunting defenses.

Pages 5, 6 and 7 — Diagrams of the Colts' blitzes.

If there was one thing the Jets wanted to encourage the Colts to do, it was to blitz.

"John has read every blitz this season," said Ewbank, unconsciously transposing Unitas and Namath while discussing the plan. "If they blitz, he'll pick them apart."

From News Dispatches of January 9:

Billy Ray Smith, defensive captain of the Colts, was asked for an opinion on Joe Namath.

"The man can throw a football into a teacup at fifty yards," he said. "But he hasn't seen defenses like ours in his league. Our defenses are as complicated as some team's offenses. We have twenty variations of our blitzes and five or six variations up front. That lets us do a lot of things. I think reading our defenses will be a new experience for the man.

"He's a good quarterback, but he's still a young man. When he gets a little older, he'll get humility."

That night, Joe Namath made a brief appearance at a barbecue the Jets hosted for players and their families near the pool at the motel. Then he departed with Joe Fucile, a forty-two-year-old Miami used-car-lot manager, for the Miami Springs Villa, where he would receive the Miami Touchdown Club award as the "Outstanding Football Player of 1968."

Namath accepted the award, made some perfunctory remarks about how he was accepting it for the whole team and not for himself, then said awards mean nothing unless the recipients of them win games.

Then he capped a week of psychological warfare by declaring, "We are going to win on Sunday, I guarantee you."

He threw some footballs into the crowd, signed some autographs, then got into the back seat of Fucile's turquoise Cadillac for the return trip to Fort Lauderdale. On the way, Fucile's wife, Mildred, asked Namath how he could continue playing football with such bad knees.

"I'm not so bad off," he said. "Some people don't have knees."

The next morning, the Miami *Herald* had a banner headline across the front page of its sports section that read NAMATH GUARANTEES JET VICTORY. George Sauer, Sr., the Jets' director of player personnel and father of the team's split end, was disturbed when he read it. Stopping Gerry Philbin, the team's defensive end, in the lobby of the motel, he said, "Gerry, this is really going to stir the Colts up."

Philbin said, "When all this talk started, I thought the same thing. But now I'm beginning to think it's good. The trouble with Kansas City and Oakland in the last two Super Bowls was that they kept saying how great the Packers were. They didn't want to get the Packers mad. But I think some of the players started believing it themselves. There's no way, George, this team is going to beat itself."

Later that day, Lucy and Weeb Ewbank had two visitors in room 136 — Dorothy and Johnny Unitas. The Unitases were paying a social visit and the couples chatted for about an hour — but there was no talk of football.

"I didn't even ask him how his arm was," said Ewbank later. "That wouldn't have been fair."

As the Unitases were leaving the Ocean Mile, Joe Namath came through the glass front door. Wearing a black turtleneck shirt under a black blazer, he shook hands with Unitas, who was wearing a gray business suit, white shirt, patterned tie and his crew-cut. They talked for a few minutes, shook hands again, then went their separate ways.

"He asked me how my knees were," said Namath later, "and I asked him how his arm was. Neither of us got an answer."

One of four Jets who survived the transition from the old New York Titans, Don Maynard had the reputation of being the most frugal player on the team. Once, back in New York, he had his car impounded for parking in a no-parking zone. It would cost him fifty dollars to get it back. He told Jim Hudson of the incident and, after listening to Maynard describe the New York Police Department for twenty minutes in less than flattering adjectives, Hudson finally broke through and asked him where the car was now.

"They still got it," said Maynard.

"They still got it? Three days? Why the hell don't you pick it up?"

"Because," said Maynard, "I want to get my money's worth."

Maynard, like Larry Grantham, Bill Mathis and Curley Johnson, was a survivor of the days when the Titans played in the Polo Grounds, where pigeons outnumbered fans. When players went to the bank, they looked sheepishly at tellers and hoped for the best. Titan paychecks had been known to bounce higher than unretrieved punts.

Sitting in his room at the motel on the day before the game, Maynard

The Jets' Gerry Philbin liked Namath's guarantee.

described the evolution of the Jets from the Titans.

"For nine years, I don't think anyone, with the exception of Grantham and Mathis, suffered as much frustration as I did. It was horrible — feeling unwanted, being looked down upon, being ignored by the fans and ridiculed by the press, season after season. It all began in 1960 when I reported to the Titans' first training camp. It was a new team in a new league and there were over a hundred of us trying to get a job. The NFL didn't want any of us. We were faceless. It was completely different from the year I reported to the New York Giants' camp and recognized guys like Kyle Rote and Frank Gifford and Charley Conerly. Nobody recognized anybody at that first camp with the Titans.

"I never had a feeling of belonging that summer until one of the older players, Bobby Dillon, came over to me after we played an exhibition game in Bangor, Maine, and shook my hand and welcomed me to the team. It was like the President shaking my hand. Nobody remembers Bobby, but I'll never forget him for what he did.

"When Bobby was let go, I became friends with Grantham and Mathis, and they were the only two friends I had. The New York fans could hardly be called our friends. The sportswriters made fun of us, and that made it even worse. The Giants had New York all to themselves then and we were treated like intruders — or worse, clowns. At most games you could count the fans in the stands. They were the smallest crowds I had ever played before.

"In our third year, 1962, I figured we reached the end of the line. Our paychecks were bouncing and I didn't know what to do. That was the first time a thing like that had ever happened to any of us. It made us do a lot of wondering about the future of the Titans and the AFL, as well. We thought that the team and the league were about to go down the drain. But the league office stepped in, paid our salaries and assured us that everything would be all right. When the season ended we didn't know if any of us would be back. As bad as attendance was the first two years, the third year it was even worse. Personally, I didn't think there would be a New York Titan team the next season — I knew the club would have to be sold, and I was figuring that whoever bought it would move it to another city. I remember shaking hands with my teammates and wondering if I'd ever see them again.

"I was back home in Texas the following March when I heard the Titans had been sold to a group of businessmen headed by Sonny Werblin. I had never heard of Werblin, and the only things I could find out were that the club would stay in New York and that the name would be changed from Titans. I was ready to quit football. The thought of going back to the Polo Grounds to play for a bunch of new owners I knew nothing about didn't appeal to me at all.

John Unitas was called the master, but he had been injured most of the year.

"A couple weeks later I read where Weeb Ewbank had been named head coach and that changed my mind. I didn't know him personally, but I read a lot about him from his days in Baltimore. I was sold on the fact that the new owners were taking football seriously. So when I got to the first Jet training camp in 1963 in Peekskill, New York, I was eager for a fresh start. Most of the old Titans were still around, but it didn't take long to get the feeling of not belonging all over again. Ewbank made a statement that he would eventually get rid of all the old Titans. It gave me a scared feeling right away. I didn't know whether to pack up and leave or stick around and give it a shot. Finally, Grantham and I had a long talk and we decided to stay. The hell with them, we thought, we're pros and we're going to show them. But I had that feeling of having to prove myself all over again.

"There was a lot of friction in that first Jet camp. Every day a couple of old Titans were cut from the team and a couple of ex-Colts would arrive to take their places. All the ex-Colts stuck together and all the old Titans stuck together. We felt we were the underdogs because we knew the front office wanted a new image. The fewer old Titans around, the better everybody would like it. During practices I felt I was an open target for criticism by the coaches simply because I was an old Titan. A quarterback would throw a pass over my head or behind me and I would be the one they screamed at. I was going to pack it in again, but this time George Sauer, the only holdover coach from the Titans, talked me out of it.

"That season a lot more people came out to see us play and Werblin organized things so well that, for the first time, I had confidence in the front office. The next year, we moved into Shea Stadium and it was like another world. The fans really started coming out and we drew more people in the first season at Shea than we had in three years at the Polo Grounds combined. That first year at Shea, Matt Snell was the best rookie in the league. He gave us the running attack we needed so badly. Now all we needed was a quarterback. Werblin went out and got us Joe Namath.

"There were a lot of stories going around about Joe and his $400,000 contract, stories that implied a lot of us resented Joe because of the money he got. They were blown up out of proportion. I, for one, never resented a dime of it. I felt that if a player could get that kind of money, I was all for it. A lot of other guys were grumbling, though, about management. They figured if the club could afford to give that kind of money to a rookie, it should spread a little more around to the veterans.

"I had a great understanding with Joe right from the start. I told him privately, 'If anything doesn't work out in a game, let's you and me talk it over.' I respect quarterbacks and I promised him, 'You make me look good and I'll make you look good. I don't want you shaking your head and turning your back, and me talking to myself.' Joe agreed with me and right off the

Joe Namath on the day before the game.

THE OPENING MATCHUPS

NEW YORK ON OFFENSE

No.	Player	Ht.	Wt.	Pos.
13	Don Maynard	6-1	179	WR
83	George Sauer	6-2	195	WR
87	Pete Lammons	6-3	233	TE
67	Dave Herman	6-1	255	RT
66	Randy Rasmussen	6-2	255	RG
52	John Schmitt	6-4	245	C
61	Bob Talamini	6-1	255	LG
75	Winston Hill	6-4	280	LT
12	Joe Namath	6-2	195	QB
32	Emerson Boozer	5-11	202	RB
41	Matt Snell	6-2	219	FB

BALTIMORE ON DEFENSE

No.	Player	Ht.	Wt.	Pos.
43	Lenny Lyles	6-2	204	RCB
40	Bob Boyd	5-10	192	LCB
20	Jerry Logan	6-1	190	SS
78	Bubba Smith	6-7	295	LE
74	Billy Ray Smith	6-4	250	LT
53	Dennis Gaubatz	6-2	232	MLB
76	Fred Miller	6-3	250	RT
81	Ordell Braase	6-4	245	RE
21	Rick Volk	6-3	195	FS
32	Mike Curtis	6-2	232	LLB
66	Don Shinnick	6-0	228	RLB

BALTIMORE ON OFFENSE

No.	Player	Ht.	Wt.	Pos.
87	Willie Richardson	6-2	198	WR
28	Jimmy Orr	5-11	185	WR
88	John Mackey	6-2	224	TE
73	Sam Ball	6-4	240	RT
71	Dan Sullivan	6-3	250	RG
50	Bill Curry	6-2	235	C
62	Glenn Ressler	6-3	250	LG
72	Bob Vogel	6-5	250	LT
15	Earl Morrall	6-2	206	QB
41	Tom Matte	6-0	214	RB
45	Jerry Hill	5-11	215	FB

NEW YORK ON DEFENSE

No.	Player	Ht.	Wt.	Pos.
42	Randy Beverly	5-11	198	RCB
24	Johnny Sample	6-1	204	LCB
22	Jim Hudson	6-2	210	SS
81	Gerry Philbin	6-2	245	LE
72	Paul Rochester	6-2	250	LT
62	Al Atkinson	6-2	230	MLB
80	John Elliott	6-4	249	RT
86	Verlon Biggs	6-4	268	RE
46	Bill Baird	5-10	180	FS
51	Ralph Baker	6-3	235	LLB
60	Larry Grantham	6-0	212	RLB

bat we hit it off. There was no bullshit, we just laid it on the line to each other."

That night, both teams enforced rigid curfews. The Jets had a buffet snack at the hotel and all players were instructed to be tucked into their rooms by 11 P.M., at which time the coaches would conduct a bed check of those not staying with their wives. Missing a bed check on the night before the Super Bowl would cost a guilty Jet a fine of five thousand dollars. Any Colt not responding to the bed check would be suspended from playing in the game.

Namath answered the eleven-o'clock knock on his door in his undershorts, told Clive Rush, the offensive coach, that he was going to stay up for a while to look at color movies of the Colts, and Rush said, "Fine. If you detect anything new let me know about it right away."

If anything new did show up in Namath's room that night he did not rush to tell Rush about it.

At the Orange Bowl on game day, the crowd started arriving around noon for the 3:05 P.M. kickoff. The morning had started with a drizzle but the sun was melting the clouds and starting to break through them. The Jets would dress in the Miami Dolphins' locker room, the Colts in the visiting team locker room. But before the teams arrived, the Miami Beach Police Department's bomb squad pulled up in its bomb-disposal truck. At police headquarters earlier in the morning, a telephone caller said that a bomb had been planted in the stadium. Before anyone could be admitted, the stadium had to be searched. It was, and nothing was found resembling a bomb.

Arriving with the mere mortals, many of whom wore Maurice Chevalier straw hats, were the socio-political luminaries: President-elect Richard Nixon; Vice-President-elect Spiro Agnew, a devout Colt fan; Senator Edward Kennedy of Massachusetts and his father, former Ambassador Joseph P. Kennedy; Senator William Eastland of Mississippi; governors Claude Kirk of Florida and James Rhodes of Ohio; astronauts Frank Borman, Bill Anders and Jim Lovell. Comedians Bob Hope and Jackie Gleason were less than conspicuous sitting on opposite sides of the field.

In the catacombs of the stadium, the Colts and Jets were dressing, the Colts in blue jerseys and the Jets in white.

In the Colts' locker room, Shula was walking around telling each of his players, "Don't wait for them to lose it. We've got to win it ourselves."

In the Jet locker room, George Sauer, Jr., was lying on his back, holding up his ankles. "I'm pretending I'm a frog layin' on its back," he said.

Namath, clad only in a jockstrap, was in the latrine shaving. Jim Turner, the place-kicker, was in a nearby toilet stall, throwing up.

A half hour before kickoff, Referee Tommy Bell signaled both benches to send their captains to midfield for the coin toss. Since Namath, the offensive captain, was busy warming up on the sidelines, Ewbank sent Johnny Sample, the defensive captain, out to the 50-yard line. Bell and Sample's old friend, Lenny Lyles, one of the Colts' captains, were waiting for Sample.

"You don't have to introduce us," Sample said to Bell.

"All right, Captain Sample," said Bell, "the Jets are the visiting team. Wait until the coin is in the air and call it loud."

Bell flipped the silver dollar into the air and Sample called heads.

"Heads it is," said Bell.

Sample informed him that the Jets would receive and then, before departing, said to Lyles, "The first one goes to us."

After Lou Michaels kicked off for Baltimore, Namath quickly revealed his operating plan — establish a running game first so the passes would work later. He sent Snell over Bob Talamini at left guard for three yards, then sent Snell over Winston Hill at left tackle for nine more. On that play, Rick Volk, a Baltimore safety, came up to stop Snell and met him head-on. Volk did not get up. The impact had knocked him virtually unconscious and he had to be helped off the field. In two plays, Matt Snell, for all practical purposes, established a running game for the Jets.

The Colts stopped that series, however, and got the ball. Earl Morrall mixed his plays well, passing to John Mackey and alternating Tom Matte and Jerry Hill on running plays. The Colts were moving so well, it appeared as if Jimmy (The Greek) Snyder had short-changed them as only eighteen-point favorites. But the drive finally sputtered on the New York 27-yard line. Lou Michaels came onto the field to kick a field goal, with Morrall holding. His kick was wide of the goalposts and, as the Colts headed for the sidelines shaking their horseshoed heads, the Jets' offense became aroused.

Namath moved the Jets well again, but Sauer fumbled a pass and Baltimore's Ron Porter recovered on the Jets' 12-yard line. It looked as if Baltimore would surely score from there. As the first period ended, the Colts were on the Jets' 6-yard line. Morrall, on the second play of the second period, dropped back to pass and spotted Tom Mitchell alone in a corner of the end zone and threw to him. But Al Atkinson, the Jets' middle line-backer, tipped it with his right hand and the ball fell into the hands of Randy Beverly, the Jets' safety whom Mitchell had eluded. The Colts, after two easy chances to score, had nothing to show for them.

The Jets, aroused, along with the crowd, took over on their own 20,

With Bill Mathis blocking, Matt Snell picks up yardage on the Colts.

George Sauer's reception set up the first Jet touchdown.

and Namath marched them downfield like a shepherd moves his flock. When Sauer caught a pass and ran it eleven yards to the Baltimore 23, the Colts' defense was frustrated.

"I could hear them cursing themselves in their huddle," John Schmitt, the Jets' center, would say later. "They were mad as hell that we were moving."

The Jets got it down to the Colts' 4-yard line, where Namath called a "19-Option." He handed off to Snell, who went through the left side of the Colts' line and into the end zone. Jim Turner kicked the extra point and, for the first time in the history of the Super Bowl, the AFL was ahead, 7–0.

Just before the end of the first half, the Colts had a chance to tie it. The Colts took over on the Jets' 42 with forty-three seconds remaining. Morrall threw a screen pass to Jerry Hill that went nowhere. From the sidelines, Shula called for the "flea-flicker." Morrall handed off to Tom Matte, who headed right, stopped, turned and lateraled back to Morrall. Looking for receivers down the middle, Morrall failed to see Jimmy Orr in the left corner of the Jets' end zone, waving his arms, all alone. He threw instead to Hill — a floater — and Jim Hudson intercepted it for New York. End of Colt opportunity, end of first half.

"I heard Jimmy screaming as we headed for the locker room," said Morrall. "He was screaming, 'Didn't you see me, Earl? Didn't you see me?' I told him, 'No, Jimmy, I didn't.' I had to turn to my right in order to take the pass from Matte and when I looked up, Jimmy wasn't in my line of vision. Jerry Hill was, so I went to him.

"I couldn't believe our luck was so bad. I kept asking myself, 'What's happening? What do we have to do?' I knew the Jets were fired up now and I could see the crowd shifting its allegiance to them. Namath was becoming the dragon-slayer just like he said he would, and I just couldn't believe that. The pass Beverly intercepted was the turning point in the first half. If we would have scored then, we wouldn't have been so frustrated. The ironic part of it was that Beverly, the hero, was so faked out of position, it was unbelievable. The whole complexion of the game changed in those few seconds. I was beginning to think that the stars were against us or something.

"When we got together in the locker room, Shula started to talk, and he was hot. I had seen him like this only a couple times before, once during the Atlanta game we almost gave away and again when we played Cleveland in the regular season, a game we eventually lost. He was saying, 'We're making stupid mistakes, we're stopping ourselves. You've got them believing in themselves. You've got them believing they're better than we are.' It lasted three or four minutes and it really got us mad. We went out on the field for the second half with fire pouring out of our eyes."

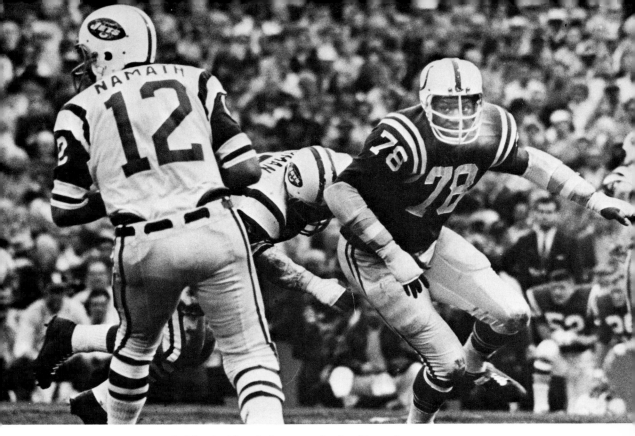

Bubba Smith only has eyes for Joe Namath.

Randy Beverly's interception was a turning point.

Incensed over missed opportunities that could have produced as many as twenty-seven points in the first half, Shula had made a decision at half time that he would keep to himself — he was giving Morrall one series to accomplish something. If he failed, Unitas would take over at quarterback.

Walking onto the field, Shula turned to one of his assistants and said, "Damn it, the flea-flicker is designed especially for Orr. Morrall's supposed to look for him. Whatinhell is happening?"

The Colts received the second-half kickoff and, on the very first play from scrimmage, Tom Matte fumbled and Ralph Baker recovered for the Jets on Baltimore's 33. Morrall hadn't had the opportunity to achieve anything, so the fumble gave him a second chance -- or, to Shula's way of thinking — delayed his departure.

In five plays the Jets' deepest penetration was to the Colts' 11, but they wound up losing ground and having to settle for a 32-yard field goal by Turner for a 10–0 lead.

The Colts got the ball again and, in three plays, Morrall overthrew Mackey, got no yardage on a pass to Hill and lost two yards when he was chased from the pocket. The Jets got the ball and moved to the Colts' 23, and Turner kicked another field goal for a 13–0 lead.

"Shula was waiting for me as I came off the field," said Morrall. "He said, 'I'm going to put John in. I'm going to give him a chance. We've got to get rolling.' I nodded, that's all. Earlier in the year against Cleveland the team was flat and Shula put Unitas in to start the third quarter. I really boiled. But not this time. It wasn't hard to take. If I was a coach and my team was being quarterbacked by a guy who couldn't get the ball over the goal line, then I'd sure as hell do something. But we were losing our poise and our self-assurance was beginning to drain away, little by little, like beans trickling out of the bottom of a torn sack. It was sad."

Unitas, after a season of arm trouble, took over and did nothing. The Colts punted on what would be their last play of the third period — a period in which they managed only seven offensive plays for a net ten yards.

With just over thirteen minutes left in the game, Turner kicked another field goal for the Jets, making it 16–0. The 75,377 spectators and many in the television audience of sixty million viewers were in shock, not to mention the Baltimore Colts. The frustration of the Colts was starting to show itself in a less than diplomatic manner.

After Willie Richardson of the Colts went out of bounds with a pass, Johnny Sample of the Jets, covering him, barrelled into a cluster of players near the Baltimore bench. Before Sample could get back on the field, Tom Mitchell, the tight end who had had a touchdown pass taken from him by Beverly early in the game, ran up to Sample and swung his empty helmet

John Unitas came off the bench in the third quarter.

Johnny Sample wrestles down Colts' Willie Richardson.

across Sample's head. Sample flared out at him but, considering the odds, returned to the field, his ears ringing.

A few minutes later, Beverly intercepted another pass, a weak floater by Unitas intended for Orr, and Sample leaped into the air and slapped the back of Tom Matte's helmet. "It looks bad, buddy," Sample said.

Matte went after Sample, who was running toward the Jets' bench. Sample stopped to encounter him. But before a fistfight could erupt, game officials moved between them and broke it up.

Namath, calling a succession of running plays to eat time, moved to the Colts' 42, from where Turner missed a forty-nine-yard field-goal attempt. With 6:34 left, Unitas came back on the field in an attempt to avert the embarrassment of being shut out by an American Football League team. He succeeded — with less than four minutes left, Jerry Hill scored from the 1-yard line and Michaels kicked the extra point. It would stand at 16–7 to the end, despite some desperate — and unsuccessful — maneuvering by the Colts.

As the game ended, Ewbank was carried off the field and Namath, accompanied by the roar of the crowd, ran toward the locker room, his right arm raised into the air and his index finger pointed skyward, borrowing the college symbol for being No. 1.

Ewbank and Shula met at midfield, seconds after the final gun.
"We got all the breaks," Ewbank said.
"Your team played well," answered Shula.
"Nice of you to say that," said Ewbank, and they both departed into the hysterical mass of humanity surrounding them.

In the locker room, Johnny Sample was holding court:
"It'll take the NFL twenty years to catch us. . . ."
"They panicked, they were so shaken up they forgot the game plan. That's why Shula benched Morrall. . . ."
"Kansas City and Oakland are better than the Colts. . . ."
"We're the greatest team ever, better than the 1958 and 1959 Colt teams I played on. . . ."

In another corner, Ralph Baker, the linebacker, waited for newsmen to come his way. When they did, he said, "Hey, you guys hear the latest? We've just been made fourteen-point underdogs to the College All-Stars."

Namath was informed he was the winner of the *Sport* magazine Dodge Charger as the game's Most Valuable Player.

Al Atkinson restrains Tom Matte from going after Johnny Sample.

"That one of those you keep for a year?" he asked.

"No, it's yours to keep," he was told.

"That's more like it," he smiled.

A newsman asked Joe if he felt sorry for Earl Morrall.

"Better him than me."

Ewbank, after a dunk in the shower, came out dripping. A newsman asked him what he had to say for himself?

"I'm all wet."

The Colts dressed quickly and had nothing worth reporting to say. They were responding with clichés to obvious human questions. Nobody mentioned the frustration and the embarrassment; nobody mentioned the dissatisfaction with Earl Morrall; nobody mentioned how the Jets had been underestimated.

But when they arrived back at the Sheraton-Hilton, a more serious problem was developing. Rick Volk, who had been the victim of a head-on collision with Matt Snell on the second play of the game and had to be carried off the field later, was lying unconscious in the bathroom of his room and his wife, Charlene, was running down the hall, screaming for a doctor. Volk was vomiting, his body was quivering in convulsions and he was swallowing his tongue.

Fortunately, Dr. Norman Freeman, the team physician, was a few rooms away, checking on Dennis Gaubatz, a linebacker. He used a ballpoint pen to free Volk's tongue, summoned an ambulance and took him to the emergency room of Holy Cross Hospital. At the hospital, Volk regained consciousness and was placed under intensive care. An examination by a neurosurgeon revealed no serious damage.

"The vomiting," said Dr. Freeman, "increased the inter-cranial pressure, causing the convulsions."

Volk looked up at his wife and asked, "Who won?"

When Namath returned to the Governor's Suite at the Gault Motel, a dozen red roses were waiting for him. They had been delivered by a local florist just after the game began. There was no card attached, but the front desk told Namath the roses had been sent by "a Mister Lou Michaels of the Baltimore Colts."

On the day after the game, there was subdued joy in Namath's home-town of Beaver Falls, a community of 16,240 people thirty miles north of Pittsburgh that had had little else to become excited about during the previous twelve months: The Brodhead Hotel went out of business after forty-two

Joe Namath's locker-room flankers: Coach Ewbank and Joe's dad.

years as a local landmark; the school board in neighboring Patterson Township got mutinous and threatened to form a school district of its own; the big centennial celebration was nearly spoiled by a squabble over who the city's first World War II casualty *really* was. Then the high school football team went out and lost two of its ten games and the season was immediately written off as a disaster. "Only God and family," said Joe Tronzo, sports editor of the Beaver Falls *News-Tribune,* "have higher priorities than winning football games in Beaver Falls. But yesterday was the day that seemed to bring the town together. The streets were deserted. Everybody was home, watching the game. If some crook was smart, he'd have come in and cleaned this town out yesterday afternoon."

If Namath's success in the Super Bowl had an effect on Beaver Falls, it was hardly apparent. The town seemed to flow to its normal phlegmatic gait as soon as the whistles shrieked, signaling the end of another working day in the nearby steel mills. Over at Rio's Grill on Seventh Avenue, steelworkers gathered for short beers and tall tales while munching on sixty-five-cent roast beef sandwiches, and over at John Gregory's Barber Shop on Eighth Avenue, world problems were discussed and solutions found in the fifteen minutes it took John Gregory to give a trim. As one of the last bastions of hat-tipping gentlemen and no-tipping restaurants, one could hardly accuse Beaver Falls of being the birthplace of someone as ebullient as Joe Namath. Wayne Morse or Andy Griffith, yes; but not Willie White Shoes himself.

"A lot of folks around town don't like Joe," said Tronzo, who once ran for mayor (and lost). "They think he's a wise guy and they remember when he was in school. He had a lotta trouble with teachers. He'd answer them back, things like that. A lot of teachers accused Larry Bruno, the football coach, of protecting Joe and letting him get away with murder. Larry didn't really protect Joe, he just did a lot of bending with him. But Larry's that kind of guy.

"I had to give Joe hell the last time I saw him. He was at his mother's house for a visit and I told him, 'Hey, Joe, what is this stuff about Bear this and Bear that? Why are you always falling over Bear Bryant? Don't you know the guy who put you on your way was Larry Bruno? Why don't you give Larry some credit once in a while? You know where you'd be without him?' Joe just nodded and said, 'Yeah, you're right.'"

On this day after Super Bowl III, there were people in Beaver Falls speaking reverently of Namath, but one could only speculate on just how much his success in football had tempered their tones. With what degree of tolerance were the cute little stories of Namath mischief transmitted a decade earlier? Over at Rio's, where Namath stops frequently when he's in town (and tips bartender Jack Sheridan two dollars for a night's work), the legends of Namath's boyhood were flowing as freely as the draft beer.

Joe Namath, prankster:

"Right after Joe's Beaver Falls High School football team won the league title," said Bill Ross, the school's athletic director, "Joe climbed on the roof of the Sahli Chevrolet building on Seventh Avenue and shinnied up the flag pole. He wanted to tie an orange balloon on the top, advertising the team's championship. Well, a crowd started to gather and the police were called and Joe, as usual, got in a helluva mess."

Joe Namath, individualist:

"Joe was a pretty good high school basketball player," said Tronzo. "But one day he got mad about something in practice and walked off the court. Coach Nate Lippe had no choice but to throw him off the team."

Joe Namath, mystery man:

"Joe was all set to go to Maryland," said Bruno, his high school coach. "He just missed a 750 total score on his college boards and was going to try again. Then, in the middle of the summer, he disappeared. Nobody knew where he went. Finally, after a few days, I got a long-distance call from Tuscaloosa, Alabama. It was Joe. 'Coach,' he said, 'I'm going to play for Bear Bryant.'"

Across the Beaver River in New Brighton, on the corner of Third Avenue and Eleventh Street, Irving Laine owned and operated a pharmacy. He had one employee, a quiet woman who wore dark-rimmed glasses and greeted customers cheerfully with a shy smile. Her name was Rose Szolnoki, and she is Joe Namath's mother.

"I started working here a few months ago to keep myself busy," she said. "Sitting around the house all day was making me nervous. A lot of people probably think it's terrible that Joe Namath's mother works in a drugstore. But I'm happy and that's what matters. I'm working because I want to, not because I have to."

Later, in her one-family white house at 1604 Ross Hill overlooking the city, Rose Szolnoki said she was worried about her youngest son. "I want Joey to quit. I don't want him playing football anymore. I don't want his knees to hurt again. I don't want him crippled."

Rose Szolnoki said she had watched the Super Bowl game the previous day on television, sticking to her usual ritual of lighting religious candles and praying.

"I pray to one saint when Joey has the ball, and to another one when the other team has it. Joey got a big kick out of it when I told him I always do it. He said I had an offensive saint and a defensive saint. He's always making cracks like that, but some of them, I guess, get him into trouble. He doesn't mean anything by them. That's just Joey, and he's a good boy.

"My Joey used to be an altarboy once, you know."

So, after the surprise outcome of Super Bowl III became gray with the passing of time and newsprint, a sober evaluation of the game left one question lingering: What did it all prove?

First, it made the Super Bowl a legitimate national sports attraction after two straight mismatches. Second, it put the American Football League on an equal level with the National, after eight years, and made the forthcoming merger more palatable for both sides. And it made Joe Namath the folk hero of American sports, less than what most traditionalists would have liked, perhaps; but superficially more acceptable to them than his predecessor, Muhammad Ali, who was stinging and floating in limbo, his title taken from him, for refusing to be drafted.

Super Bowl III changed the attitudes of an entire nation of fans toward a league and its showcase player. For that reason alone, it may have been the most important single professional football game ever played. Certainly, it was the most important of the 1960's.

Joe Namath and Johnny Sample join Mayor Lindsay at New York's City Hall.

SUPER BOWL IV

HAIL TO THE CHIEF

Participants — Kansas City Chiefs, champions of the American Football League, and Minnesota Vikings, champions of the National Football League.

Date — January 11, 1970.

Site — Tulane Stadium, New Orleans, Louisiana.

Time — 2:35 P.M., CST.

Attendance — 80,998.

Radio and Television — Columbia Broadcasting System (TV and Radio).

Regular-Season Records — Kansas City, 11-3; Minnesota, 12-2.

Playoff Records — Kansas City defeated Oakland Raiders, 17-7, for AFL title; Minnesota defeated Cleveland Browns, 27-7, for NFL title.

Players' Shares — $15,000 to each member of winning team; $7,500 to each member of losing team.

Gate Receipts — Estimated $800,000.

Radio-TV Receipts — $2,500,000.

Officials — Referee, John McDonough; Umpire, Lou Pilazzi; Head Linesman, Harry Kessel; Line Judge, Bill Schleibaum; Back Judge, Tom Kelleher; Field Judge, Charlie Musser.

Coaches — Hank Stram, Kansas City; Bud Grant, Minnesota.

From the Huntley-Brinkley Report, *NBC-TV, January 6:*

> In Detroit, a special Justice Department Task Force conducting what it described as the "biggest gambling investigation of its kind ever," is about to call seven professional football players and one college head coach to testify on their relationships with known gamblers, most notably Donald (Dice) Dawson of Detroit, who was arrested on New Year's Day with $450,000 in checks and gambling records on him. Among the players scheduled to appear is Len Dawson, quarterback for the Kansas City Chiefs, who will play the Minnesota Vikings in the Super Bowl Sunday.

"I spent two weeks digging out the story," said Bill Matney, Midwest correspondent for the National Broadcasting Company. "The first tip came into NBC's Washington bureau, and I happened to be there at the time. For a week we worked on it but got nowhere. Then I flew back to Chicago, where I was based, and spent the next few days on the telephone calling contacts in Detroit, where the task force was based. Since I used to work in Detroit for a newspaper, I started making some headway. When I reached a contact right inside the task force itself who was willing to give me some names and information, I jumped on a plane, flew to Detroit and met him in person. He was more than cooperative — he gave me a list of all the football people who were going to be questioned, and there were more than eight names on it, about fifty altogether. But he circled eight and said, 'These people will be called for sure.'

"Since the guy was working on the investigation himself, I had to consider him an unimpeachable source. I called NBC in New York and the people in the news department told me to double- and triple-check everything to make sure there were no doubts in my mind about it. So I went to see an old friend of mine, Jim Brickley, who was the United States Attorney. We had a secret meeting and I told him what I had uncovered. He was shocked but tried to cover it up by being cool about it. He said he didn't know any of the names on the list and that he couldn't confirm or deny it. Since the task force was operating as a separate entity, I assumed — quite correctly — that it just hadn't gotten around to giving Brickley the names.

"I was convinced in my own mind that all eight were going to be called to testify. I was aware that the Super Bowl was only a week away, and I knew what would happen when Lenny Dawson's name went around the country as being connected with a gambling investigation. But there was no way I was going to cop out. It was a story I worked hard to uncover and, Super Bowl or not, I felt it was worth reporting. I called NBC back and said I was ready with all the details and that there was no doubt in my mind that everything was accurate and factual. The New York bureau said, 'All right, we go with it on Tuesday.'

"I broke the story on Detroit Station WWJ-TV on its six-o'clock news program. A half hour later the *Huntley-Brinkley Report* led off its program with the fact that the task force had been in operation in Michigan and had uncovered the names of at least eight people in football who were going to be called to testify. Then it switched to me in Detroit for the details.

"Within hours after the program, there were wire reports saying that Len Dawson and Bill Munson of the Detroit Lions, who also was among the eight, admitted knowing Dice Dawson. I got a call from the Washington bureau and one of the guys in the office said that Attorney General John Mitchell was 'furious.' Then I got a call from my source. He said two things were happening: One, that Mitchell had ordered an investigation within the department to find out who leaked the information and, two, the task force was going to be forced to change its *modus operandi*. Instead of calling the players to testify in person, it was going to dispatch agents to see them, avoiding any appearances in court. The signed depositions would take the place of sworn testimony.

"The football people were saying that I was irresponsible and the Justice Department was mad as hell. But I don't work for either of them. NBC said it was a helluva story. I knew I had the facts right, and I knew they were accurate. To hold off until after the Super Bowl game, on the premise that it might hurt Len Dawson's performance, would have been the most flagrant form of journalistic weakness."

While Matney's report was being carried across the country, the Chiefs were sequestered in the Fontainebleau Hotel on Tulane Avenue in New Orleans. Those who heard it on television reacted as if some unknown force had swooped into their lair, terrorized the whole team for a few seconds and then flown off with their quarterback in its grasp. The Chiefs, like all pro football teams, were hypersensitive to gambling rumors; less than six months earlier the commissioner of football, Pete Rozelle, had ordered Joe Namath of the New York Jets to sell his interest in a bar, Bachelors III, on New York's East Side, because it was being frequented by gamblers or, at least, men who were suspected of being gamblers. Namath, ever the individualist, responded by emotionally announcing his retirement, denying any contact with gamblers and refusing to sell his share of the bistro. But he and Rozelle finally solved the matter, privately, and Rozelle's message was obvious: Under no circumstances will the integrity of the game be placed in jeopardy by players' friendships with gamblers, or suspected gamblers.

After Paul Hornung of the Green Bay Packers and Alex Karras of the Detroit Lions were suspended for a year by Rozelle for betting on games — albeit their own — Rozelle beefed up the league's security force and made its top priority the investigation of any relationship between a player and a known or suspected gambler. It was as if Rozelle were telling any neophyte fan harboring suspicion, "Look, I'm more concerned about the honesty of this game than anything else. Stick with me and we'll weed out the potential problems and football will be as clean as a hound's tooth forever." Rozelle then adopted a split stance: 1) He put a tail on players who frequented establishments patronized by gamblers, and 2) he put on a smiling public face and pretended that the only betting on football games in America were nickel-and-dime friendly wagers. Actually, with the exception of horseracing, no sport in the country inspired more betting than pro football, with its point spreads, sore knees and aching arms and frequent attractive pairings that whetted appetites.

Len Dawson and the Kansas City Chiefs had been the gambling route before. In 1968, rumors had drifted up to Rozelle's offices, on the twelfth floor of 410 Park Avenue in New York, that the Chiefs were involved in something unusual. The Chiefs, it seemed, were being taken "off the boards" every week — meaning bookies would not accept bets on their games on the suspicion that the games were fixed. Rozelle conducted an immediate inquiry — secret, of course — and summoned Len Dawson for questioning. In the process, Dawson volunteered to submit to a lie-detector test, which, presumably, he passed. Although Rozelle never revealed publicly that the investigation had been conducted, Dawson was privately cleared of any wrongdoing by him.

When Matney's televised report sent ripples through living rooms of

America, Dawson went into seclusion in his room at the Fontainebleau. His roommate, corner back Johnny Robinson, fended off all incoming calls and visitors by stating in a voice usually reserved for opposing wide receivers, "Leave the guy alone."

Unfortunately for the Chiefs — but fortunately, it seemed, for the working press — a news conference had been scheduled long in advance for the following morning at eleven at the Fontainebleau. Hank Stram, coach of the Chiefs, arrived with an ashen-faced, somber Len Dawson, who was immediately asked the questions he was expecting.

"Yes, I knew Donald Dawson. . . . Met him ten years ago. . . . The only conversations I've had with him in recent years concerned my knee injury and the death of my father. . . . No, I've never had any business dealings with him. . . . The only contact I've had with Dawson was by telephone or an occasional personal meeting. . . . Yes, I'm shocked by all of this. . . . No, I'm not going to elaborate on my relationship with Donald Dawson. . . . Are we going to get into all of this?"

Stram, standing alongside his quarterback, admonished the press, "Gentlemen, please. We'd like to keep this on the football game."

Later, Stram said that Dawson had read a statement to his teammates at a team breakfast meeting, revealing to them for the first time that he had taken a lie-detector test in 1968 and been found innocent. The players, Stram said, had no reason to question Dawson's integrity. Jerry Mays, defensive left end, said, "Lenny got a big hand when he got up, like a speaker at a banquet. He read his statement and Stram said, 'Are there any questions about this?' Just like he would do at any other meeting. Nobody responded, so Stram said, 'Any questions about anything?' E. J. Holub raised his hand. 'Yeah,' he said, 'our tickets come in yet?'"

As the Chiefs wandered in the lobby of the Fontainebleau later in the day, reporters asked them if the gambling report would have any effect on the team on Sunday?

"None at all," said Johnny Robinson. "The whole thing is ridiculous."

"We laughed about it," said Mike Garrett, the running back. "It won't affect us a single bit."

"It doesn't bother me," said Willie Lanier, the middle linebacker. "The Justice Department is doing its job. It won't add to our incentive. The incentive is being here."

"We're closer as a team now than we've ever been," said Mays.

> *DETROIT, Jan. 7 (AP) — A Justice Department spokesman said today that witnesses who were called before the Federal Grand Jury investigating nationwide gambling in sports probably would not be indicted.*
> *"The Justice Department clearly prohibits calling*

anyone as a witness when there is an indication that you are going to indict him," the spokesman said.

James Ritche, head of the Justice Department task force handling the gambling inquiry, said here that the persons called to appear before the Grand Jury were more likely to be "prospective witnesses than prospective defendants."

In the lobby of the Hilton Hotel, across from the New Orleans airport, the Minnesota Vikings, thirteen-and-a-half-point favorites to win the Super Bowl, according to Jimmy (The Greek) Snyder, were assembling for their usual 2 P.M. session on the New Orleans Saints' practice field. As controversy swirled around the Chiefs' hotel, the Vikings were being ignored, as if they were high-salaried celebrities who had come all the way down from Bloomington to play bit parts and extras' roles in a high-budget DeMille-Hitchcock-Zanuck movie starring somebody else.

The Vikings were an odd assortment of young men who were quite physical in games and in practices, yet polite when dealing with the public, the perfect mixture for most football fans. The team was formed in 1961, but seemed on the verge of splitting at the seams when Fran Tarkenton, the quarterback, and Norm Van Brocklin, the coach, had a falling out and departed within days of each other. To replace them, the Vikings went into the wilds of Canada and came back with a coach named Harold (Bud) Grant, icy to the point of glacierish, and a quarterback named Joe Kapp, a Chicano who preferred hitting people to avoiding them. That the Vikings were in the Super Bowl was no surprise — Grant had established himself as a Lombardi-like disciplinarian (players were even instructed to stand straight and tall during the playing of the pregame national anthem, no looking around), and the Vikings replaced the Packers as the game's most physical team. They had a slogan — "Forty for Sixty" — with which they advertised their unity (forty players together for sixty minutes).

But if Grant was the architect, Kapp was the catalyst; clearly a Norse of a different color. Physically, a cross between Joe Namath and Roman Gabriel, Kapp was less a stylist and more a combatant. If watching Namath was like watching an artist at work, watching Kapp was comparable to watching a plumber fix pipes. As the Vikings left for practice that day, Kapp was asked if he was going to guarantee a Viking victory — as Namath had guaranteed a Jet victory the year before over the Colts — and was right on the fly pattern.

"No," said Kapp, "no predictions, no guarantees. I don't think anybody can guarantee the result of a football game. There are two great football teams in this game and it will be a great match. We're going out there to rock and sock with the Chiefs . . . and may the best team win."

117

Coach Hank Stram runs interference for Len Dawson after meeting the press.

Like Kapp and Grant, several other Vikings were found in unusual places and carted off to Bloomington and put into purple uniforms with white horns. Of the original team, only Grady Alderman, an offensive tackle, and Jim Marshall, a defensive end, remained. The biggest bargain-basement find of all was Mick Tingelhoff, who somehow managed to make it through the 1962 college draft without being selected by a single pro team. But by the time the Vikings made it to the Super Bowl he was the best center in the game, All-Pro every year, however dubious the gimmick.

"I made it to the pros by pure luck," said Tingelhoff, in the Hilton lobby. "Not only were the NFL and AFL not interested in me, the Canadian league wasn't interested, either. I got my break because Harry Gilmer, a Vikings' scout, had a good memory. He had been up to Nebraska, where I played college ball, to look at one of our running backs and he remembered me. After the draft was over and I was eligible to sign as a free agent, he persuaded Van Brocklin to take a chance on me. I signed with the Vikings to become a middle linebacker. But Van Brocklin said I didn't move well enough to be a middle linebacker and made me the No. 2 center. Before that year was out I had the starting job, which was nice. But let's face it — who pays attention to centers? You go around asking fans to name five starting centers on pro teams and how many can do it? They know the quarterbacks and the running backs, maybe even the flankers and split ends — but centers? No, sir. I remember when I came into the league the only center who got any recognition at all was Jim Ringo.

"I think the key to recognition for a center is having a catchy name. Ringo. Tingelhoff. When it comes time to pick the All-Pro team, the players or whoever else sits down to make the choices say, 'Center? Let's see now . . . Who plays center? . . . There's Tingelhoff, and . . .' They wrack their brains for a while trying to think of who else plays center, and then they say, 'Okay, it's Tingelhoff. Now about left tackle . . .' That's how centers become All-Pros."

> *NEW ORLEANS, Jan. 8 (UPI) — Outside the Fontaine-bleau Hotel, where the Kansas City Chiefs are lodged, there is a large fountain against a backdrop of palm trees. But today, the water in the fountain was frozen and the palms were almost blue.*
>
> *The temperature is expected to drop to 24 degrees tonight, matching last night's reading, a record low for Jan. 7 here and the coldest night in seven years. The Weather Bureau has issued the following advice: "Protect your water pipes and your tender vegetation."*

From News Dispatches of January 8:

Jim Marshall, defensive left end for the Minnesota Vikings, sitting in

119

Joe Kapp came from the North to lead the Vikings.

his room at the Hilton Hotel in New Orleans, was asked what it was like in the Vikings' first season in 1961.

"Most of the guys were outcasts then, guys nobody else wanted. We knew we weren't going to win any championships that year. But we have evolved slowly into a championship team. The organization has selected its personnel as insightfully as any successful company would."

> WASHINGTON, Jan. 8 (UPI) — President Nixon will be honored Saturday as the Nation's No. 1 sports fan at the annual awards banquet of the Washington Touchdown Club. The club announced today that the President would be given its traditional "Mr. Sam" Trophy as the government figure who has contributed most to sports during the year. The trophy is named in honor of the late House Speaker, Sam Rayburn, of Texas.

> NEW ORLEANS, Jan. 8 (AP) — The Kansas City Chiefs were designated the home team today for the Super Bowl game on Sunday and will wear their red uniforms. The Minnesota Vikings will wear white, trimmed with purple.

From the New Orleans Times-Picayune *of January 8:*

> SWAP: Two Super Bowl tickets, sideline, for paint job or pickup truck.

> EXCHANGE: Two Super Bowl tickets for antique car in good condition.

> WILL TRADE: Two tickets to Super Bowl for a shotgun; two more for a motorbike.

> DEAL: Will trade two Super Bowl tickets for round-trip to Jamaica.

> BARGAIN: You can have my two tickets to the Super Bowl in exchange for an A.K.C. registered boxer puppy with fawn coloring.

From News Dispatches of January 9:

Joe Kapp, quarterback for the Minnesota Vikings, received the following telegram today:

GO, GO, SUPER JOE. STOP. YOU GAVE BRITISH COLUMBIA ITS FIRST AND ONLY GREY CUP. STOP. WE KNOW YOU WILL DELIVER THE SUPER BOWL TO MINNESOTA. STOP. WE'RE WITH YOU ALL THE WAY. STOP.

121

Defensive end Jim Marshall was an original Viking.

The telegram was signed by three thousand people in Vancouver, British Columbia, who contributed twenty-five cents each to have their names attached. A Vancouver radio station sponsored the telegram, and collected the $750. The balance, after cost of the wire, a spokesman said, would go to charity.

"I kept my two children home from school on Tuesday, then packed them up and came here to New Orleans," said Jackie Dawson, wife of the Kansas City quarterback. "We've got a daughter, Lisa, fifteen, and a son, Lenny, Jr., eleven, and I was afraid of what the other kids would say to them about their father and this gambling thing. Lenny, Jr., had a bad reaction to it, and he didn't even want to come down here for the Super Bowl game.

"We had a bad experience last year when the fans booed Len before the Denver game. Lenny was only ten and didn't realize that everyone doesn't love his daddy like we do. He didn't want to come here because he was afraid people would say bad things about his daddy again. I had to sit down with him and explain to him that this was the biggest moment of his dad's life. I told him, 'He wants you to be there and share it with him.' Finally, he agreed to come, but he was hardly overjoyed.

"We're staying in a different hotel from the team and I brought the kids over to see Len yesterday. Len wanted to assure them that everything was all right. Before we left I took Len aside and told him, 'Go out and kick the hell out of them.' I'm not as much a lady as he is a gentleman."

The city of New Orleans, which had done some hard bargaining to get the Super Bowl game into Tulane Stadium after two successful years — from an attendance standpoint — in Miami, was hardly a tropical setting during countdown week. It was cold, the wind gusted, and on Thursday night the temperature dropped to twenty degrees — lowest since 1871.

Undaunted, the local establishments treated the game as a warm-up for the Mardi Gras two months hence. On Friday night, police blocked off the French Quarter section of the city to automobile traffic and turned it over to frolickers. As if to make sure the visitors from Minnesota and Missouri were not taken by anything less than a first-class bistro, a brochure, *Special New Orleans Super Bowl Guide,* was published and distributed to all incoming football fans — free — pointing out, among other things, the places in which a football fan-tourist and his money can be disassociated quickly with the least amount of pain. The *Guide* begins:

What's your pleasure?

Strip joint or clip joint? Pompano Pontchartrain or hamburger? Draught beer or Sazerac? Dixieland jazz or progressive?

You name it and the odds are 8 to 5 you'll find it in New Orleans (pronounced Noo Awlins by the natives), the land of red beans and rice and everything that's nice.

New Orleans, Paris of the Americas, Gourmet's Heaven, land of the voodoo queens, Sin City, Funsville, and on Jan. 11, Super Bowl City, U.S.A. New Orleans, where even a funeral is cause for a parade, jazz band and all.

Mister, if you can't find your "thing" here in the crescent of the Mississippi, it just ain't worth doing.

If your "thing" is striptease, try catching Linda Brigette at the 500 Club. The little but well-stacked gal is something else. Depending upon her mood, she either sheds in front of the cash customers or comes on stage "au naturel." Either way, Linda proves an asset to the tourist trade.

Should you prefer your sex packaged in lovely costume, leaving a little to the imagination, then your place is the 809 Club where Chris Owens has been packing them in for a dozen years. Chris doesn't have to take her clothes off to please the customers. Her backdrop is excellent choreography, class costuming, a half-dozen Go Go dolls and a Conga Line which the patrons can join in and dance with the girls.

But Chris doesn't need such support. She could draw a crowd in a bare barn. She's 39-24-36 without assistance from silicone.

Another groovy place is the Sho-Bar, whose menu includes Ricki Corvette. Ricki is 6-foot-8 and measures 41-25-38.

Despite the detailed information, the football people seemed to be in less than partying moods, a condition attributable, no doubt, to the weather. Besides the cold and wind, the New Orleans Weather Bureau was conducting a tornado watch. As if to avoid the embarrassment of being picked up by a tornado cloud while examining the backfield of Linda Brigette, some football people decided to risk it in more comfortable surroundings — a gym. They drove to Baton Rouge to watch Pete Maravich play for LSU against Auburn.

MINNEAPOLIS, Jan. 10 (AP) — Robert Barbeau, an investigator in the Hennepon County Attorney's Office, ordered tickets for the Super Bowl game — and received $8,000 instead.

Barbeau said he arranged the purchase through an organization called Fun Unlimited of Minneapolis. When the envelope from the company arrived at his office last Thursday, a secretary opened it and found more than $8,000 in cash and checks.

Barbeau called the company and learned that a secretary had mistakenly placed a bank deposit in his envelope. A representative of Fun Unlimited brought Barbeau's tickets to him, and took the $8,000 back.

Jan Stenerud, the Kansas City place-kicker from Norway who went to Montana State University on a skiing scholarship and wound up as a football player, described the transition:

"I was messing around one day on the practice field when the football coaches saw me kicking the ball. They asked me to come out for the team. I didn't know a thing about football. I played a little soccer but no football. It's not very big in Norway. My folks back home still aren't sure of what I'm doing for a living over here. Anyway, I kicked some in college and when the Chiefs drafted me, I said, 'What the heck. Why not?'

"I don't know much about defenses or tackling people, but I know more than the average fan. I hate to think a game may depend on my kicking, but I'm always prepared for a close game. Mentally, I try to forget how important my kick may be, and concentrate on the kick itself.

"When I'm kicking I watch the ball and don't pay any attention to the rush. I kicked sixteen straight this season, which is a pro record, but I missed three in one game in New York. I guess you'd have to say there's a lot of luck involved.

"I walk around on the sidelines a lot to keep warm. The only thing about football I don't like is the cold weather. I worry about catching colds and the flu from standing around on the sidelines, and that's why I'm always walking around. Not because I'm bored; because I'm cold. My biggest thrill? I guess you'd have to say the two tackles I made in preseason against Oakland."

On the day before the game, the Chiefs did not so much as suit up. They lounged in their rooms and in the lobby of the Fontainebleau. Hank Stram said, "We never work out on the day before a game. We've found in the past that it has helped and we've stuck with it. I know a lot of clubs limber up on Saturday, but not us."

The Vikings, however, had a brief session, part of which was devoted to national-anthem drills.

"We let Milt Sunde handle it," said Grady Alderman. "He's a sergeant in the National Guard, and he told everybody how to line up evenly on the field, how to stand at attention and how not to wiggle or scratch while the anthem was being played."

The Vikings, perhaps, were aware that Commissioner Pete Rozelle was less than satisfied with the actions of players during the anthem. He went as far as naming one of his assistants, Bob Cochran, vice-president in charge of the national anthem and overseer of protocol.

After the workout, Bud Grant talked about his preparations for the Chiefs:

"It's hard to plan for a team when you've only seen them in three films. Heck, we've got nine years of Bart Starr on film. All we know about the Chiefs is that they're similar to the Dallas Cowboys in their style. Some friends of mine have been watching the Chiefs for quite some time. I know you're not supposed to have anybody officially scouting for you, but these friends are good friends . . . NFL friends."

Johnny Robinson, Kansas City safetyman who had been bothered all week by bruised ribs, was asked how Len Dawson was doing in the wake of the gambling reports.

"Lenny said he's never been through anything like it," said Robinson. "I know it hit him real hard. It ate him up inside, and it looked to me as if he aged five years from Tuesday to Thursday. But yesterday he got some telegrams from friends and seemed to snap out of it."

That night, less than twenty-four hours before kickoff, the Weather Bureau issued a tornado warning for Louisiana that seemed to deflate the value of game tickets from fifteen dollars each to virtually nothing. Whereas earlier in the week tickets were being traded for an assortment of valuables, on Saturday night a pair of 40-yard-line seats could be obtained for two Ramos gin fizzes.

One man in a fur coat spent the night in the lobby of a midtown hotel barking, "Super Bowl tickets — three bucks each. Get your tickets for only three bucks each." At a basketball game a man walked through the crowd and gave away twenty-four tickets. A cabdriver, after taking two passengers to the airport, accepted two Super Bowl tickets in lieu of the five-dollar fare. A sports editor of a weekly Minnesota newspaper was handed fifty tickets by a club official, who told him, "See if you can get rid of these." Later that night the sports editor said, "I tried. I unloaded a few, but it's tough. Awfully tough."

"Super Sunday," a term television had coined to promote not only the game but the day, putting it somewhere near Easter Sunday in the national pecking order, broke cold and cloudy. Another tornado warning was issued an hour before the game, but Tommy Walker, Director of Pageantry (the pregame and half-time shows) was not disturbed. Like an old vaudeville trouper, he said the show must go on. He did not specify successfully or not.

One of the most startling events in the history of pregame shows at football games occurred a half hour before kickoff. Two giant balloons, reminiscent of Mike Todd's "Around the World in 80 Days" advertisements, were scheduled to take off on each 30-yard line, drift out of the stadium and, hopefully, land in another part of New Orleans. Inside the balloons were men dressed in the costumes of a Viking and an Indian chief. The Viking, George Stokes, thirty-three, owner and founder of World Wide Ascensions in Fountain Valley, California, described the event that followed:

"We got to the 30-yard line, and my balloon just wasn't hot enough; it was cold out there and I needed more time. I didn't have my regular crew of assistants with me; I had a bunch of guys from New Orleans who didn't know too much about ballooning. Well, anyway, as they were moving my balloon into position, all of them let go and the balloon took off. I went up six or eight feet in the air, came down, hit the field, tipped over, took off again, hit again, tipped over again, and took off again. I had gone the length of the field and there was no place left to go — but the stands. The balloon hit one of the steel rafters, caught onto a loudspeaker pole and landed somewhere among the seats. I was mad as hell. There was no reason it should have happened, it was sheer stupidity. I'm a professional balloonist and I travel across the country every year flying out of county fairs and things like that, and that was the first time something like this ever happened to me. If I had my regular crew with me, it never would have happened. The guys down there just let go — they didn't know any better.

"Anyway, I'm hung up in the stands and the crowd's reaction shocked me. There was no sympathy, not even laughter. The crowd was ugly. It started ripping my balloon apart, tearing at it and pulling the signs off. All I could think of was the late 1700's in France when they used to have balloon launchings and charged people to watch. Lots of times when the balloon didn't take off, the people would attack it and rip it to shreds, then go after the guy inside. The crowds were agitated by the failure and took out their frustration on the balloon and the balloonist. But I'm saying to myself, 'Hell, this is two hundred years later, and this is a silly old football game. Why are these people acting this way?'

"Afterward, there were several forty-foot tears in the balloon and all the signs saying 'Vikings and Chiefs' were stolen. My balloon cost four thousand dollars and, lucky for me, I was able to repair the damage myself. I wasn't scared while I was bouncing along, but I was embarrassed, especially with a national television audience watching. But I couldn't get over the actions of the crowd, so animalistic, so violent. Heck, I made a flight into Anaheim Stadium before a California Angels' baseball game and, when I came close to hitting a light tower, the crowd fell into a hush. I could tell the people were concerned, and rooting for me to make it. But in New Orleans it was a bloodthirsty mob.

"If I learned one lesson from it all, it's never to rely on amateurs when you want a professional performance. I take a lot of pride in my work, and I said right then and there that I'd never work another job without at least one of my own people assisting me."

126

The pregame ceremonies had a tough time getting off the ground.

THE OPENING MATCHUPS

KANSAS CITY ON OFFENSE

No.	Player	Ht.	Wt.	Pos.
25	Frank Pitts	6-2	199	WR
89	Otis Taylor	6-3	215	WR
84	Fred Arbanas	6-3	240	TE
73	Dave Hill	6-5	260	RT
76	Mo Moorman	6-5	252	RG
55	E. J. Holub	6-4	236	C
71	Ed Budde	6-5	260	LG
77	Jim Tyrer	6-6	275	LT
16	Len Dawson	6-0	190	QB
21	Mike Garrett	5-9	200	RB
45	Robert Holmes	5-9	220	FB

MINNESOTA ON DEFENSE

No.	Player	Ht.	Wt.	Pos.
45	Ed Sharockman	6-0	200	RCB
46	Earsell Mackbee	6-0	195	LCB
29	Karl Kassulke	6-0	195	SS
81	Carl Eller	6-6	250	LE
77	Gary Larsen	6-5	255	LT
59	Lonnie Warwick	6-3	235	MLB
88	Alan Page	6-4	245	RT
70	Jim Marshall	6-3	247	RE
22	Paul Krause	6-3	188	FS
60	Roy Winston	5-11	226	LLB
58	Wally Hilgenberg	6-3	231	RLB

MINNESOTA ON OFFENSE

No.	Player	Ht.	Wt.	Pos.
84	Gene Washington	6-3	208	WR
80	John Henderson	6-3	190	WR
87	John Beasley	6-3	230	TE
73	Ron Yary	6-5	265	RT
64	Milt Sunde	6-2	250	RG
53	Mick Tingelhoff	6-2	237	C
63	Jim Vellone	6-3	255	LG
67	Grady Alderman	6-2	245	LT
11	Joe Kapp	6-3	208	QB
30	Bill Brown	5-11	230	RB
41	Dave Osborn	6-0	210	RB

KANSAS CITY ON DEFENSE

No.	Player	Ht.	Wt.	Pos.
18	Emmitt Thomas	6-2	192	RCB
40	Jim Marsalis	5-11	194	LCB
46	Jim Kearney	6-2	206	SS
75	Jerry Mays	6-4	252	LE
61	Curley Culp	6-1	265	LT
63	Willie Lanier	6-1	245	MLB
86	Buck Buchanan	6-7	287	RT
87	Aaron Brown	6-5	265	RE
42	John Robinson	6-1	205	FS
78	Bobby Bell	6-4	228	LLB
51	Jim Lynch	6-1	235	RLB

Stokes' mishap was only the beginning of a series of mistakes that turned the entertainment into unplanned and unwanted comedy. For the national anthem—during which the Vikings resembled palace guards standing a double shift on duty — Pat O'Brien, who once played the role of Knute Rockne in a football movie, was supposed to recite the words while Doc Severinson, finally moving out of the enormous shadow of Al Hirt, was to accompany him on the trumpet. O'Brien's microphone on the field went dead at the very beginning, however, and the first words the crowd heard were "home of the brave." Severinson, meanwhile, was somewhere around "the dawn's early light," a display of teamwork that would have presumably sent Rockne into the locker room for another blistering pep talk on unity.

With that embarrassment over, the game was about to begin — but not before three thousand pigeons, twenty thousand colored balloons and three tons of confetti were released into the air. Within minutes, only remnants of the pigeons and confetti were left to dot the stands. Super Bowl IV was about to begin, as ceremoniously as the *Titanic* sank.

> *KANSAS CITY, Jan. 11 (AP) — Kansas City streets were almost deserted at kickoff time for the Super Bowl bowl, and there were signs that nearly everybody was watching a television set somewhere.*
>
> *Kansas City Power and Light Co. said power usage had increased about 15,000,000 watts over a normal Sunday afternoon. Police received only one-fourth the usual number of calls for a Sunday morning. Only one crime was reported prior to kickoff — a bus station holdup.*
>
> *Firemen had only two minor blazes. J. W. Hubbell, a salesman from Houston, left his motel room and joined firemen watching TV at one firehouse because, "You can root a little better with people around than you can in a room by yourself."*
>
> *At St. Mary's Hospital maternity ward, no births were postponed by the kickoff. In the waiting room, Charles Bocker paced the floor between checks on his wife and glimpses of the pregame show. He said, "My wife'll have the game right in the middle of the baby." Downtown movie theaters also reported a drop of 85 percent in early Sunday afternoon admissions.*

Just before the Chiefs took the field, the telephone rang in a small anteroom adjacent to their locker room. An attendant answered it and called for Stram.

"Hank Stram of the Kansas City Chiefs?" the operator asked.

"Yes," said Stram, "that's right."

"Hold on one second, please, for the White House."

Richard Nixon, honored the night before in Washington as the nation's No. 1 sports fan, came on the line and talked to Stram for approximately three minutes. It was a curious call, considering that Nixon, as President-elect the year before, did not so much as make a brief appearance in the New York Jets' locker room in Miami after the Jets had pulled the biggest pro football upset ever by beating the Baltimore Colts. Nixon and Vice-President-elect Spiro Agnew were in the stands in the Orange Bowl that day.

"The President told me," said Stram, "to pass a message along to the team and to Lenny Dawson, particularly. He said, 'I know there is nothing to the rumors that your team was involved in early in the week. I just wanted to tell you to dismiss the rumors from your minds and go out there and play like champions.' We talked for a couple more minutes and then he said he didn't want to take up any more of my time; he knew I had a game to coach.

"I told him, 'Mister President, thank you very much for calling. It was very nice of you.' "

After the kickoff the teams spent several minutes testing and probing each other, like heavyweights in the first two rounds of a title fight. The Chiefs finally put together the first sustained march of the day as Len Dawson, showing no afterbirth from the gambling reports, moved the Chiefs from their own 17-yard line to the Vikings' 41. Stenerud came onto the field and kicked a forty-eight-yard field goal (a Super Bowl record) and Kansas City had a 3–0 lead that held up through the first period.

In the second period, Kansas City's offensive line — most notably Dave Hill on Carl Eller — held off the Vikings' front four long enough to give Dawson operating time. This time Dawson moved the Chiefs from their own 20 to the Vikings' 25, using play-action passes and the running of Mike Garrett to successfully confuse the Vikings' defense. From the Viking 25, Stenerud kicked another field goal for a 6–0 lead. Minutes later the pattern was identical — Dawson moved the Chiefs from the Viking 44 to the 18, Stenerud kicked his third field goal for 9–0 and the Vikings were getting nervous. The play before the field goal was an end-around by wide receiver Frank Pitts from the I-formation that caught the Vikings with their cleats implanted, particularly Ed Sharockman.

"He was getting frustrated," said Pitts of Sharockman. "I could tell just by the look on his face. Once downfield I put a block on him and he swung me off. He was trying to fling me to the ground and he couldn't. He knew he was missing coverage on me."

On the ensuing kickoff, Minnesota's Charlie West fumbled and the Chiefs' Remi Prudhomme recovered on the Vikings' 19. In five plays, Dawson

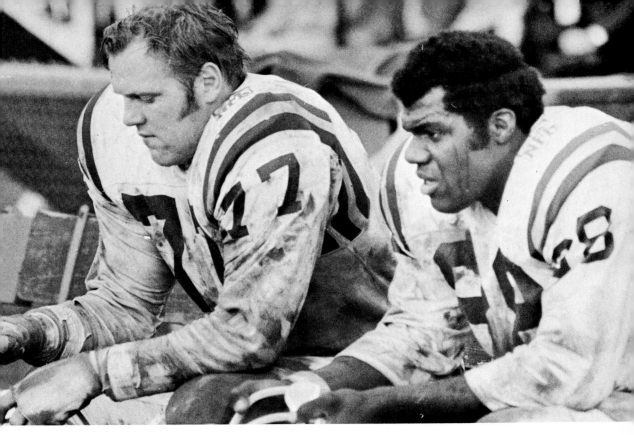

Purple People Eaters at rest: Gary Larsen, left, and Alan Page.

Frank Pitts, carrying on the end-around, plagued the Vikings.

moved it to the 5-yard line, from where Garrett ran over his left guard, Ed Budde, and into the end zone. Stenerud kicked the placement — his tenth point of the game — and the Chiefs had a 16–0 lead, which held to half time. Surprisingly, the Vikings had been ineffective in all departments: Joe Kapp couldn't get the offense moving, the front four—"The Purple People Eaters"— were being neutralized, and the team's swashbuckling spirit was not evident. And some of their tactics were hardly typical of a team that had stood so diligently during the botched national anthem — and the subtleties had not gone unnoticed by the Chiefs. Hill, a 260-pounder who had handled Eller with relative ease, was incensed at the half. "Eller was trying to hurt Lenny," he said. "He pounced on him after Lenny handed the ball off one time, and Eller knew Lenny didn't have it. That was a cheap shot and we let him know it. Another time, Alan Page punched Lenny when Lenny was down. That's high school stuff and, frankly, I'm ashamed of them for doing that."

Out on the field, Tommy Walker (Director of Pageantry) was starting the half-time show, hoping to recover the prestige that the pregame show had lost for him. Al Hirt, a part-owner of the Saints and a key figure in New Orleans' pitch to get the game — "Give us the Super Bowl and you get me free" — came out and played "Bourbon Street" as flawlessly as Gabriel might. Then came Marguerite Piazza, the opera star, singing "Basin Street Blues." *Newsday* described the rendition in one word: "mangled." That left Walker with a .500 average, but he had a chance to raise it considerably with a successful re-creation of the "Battle of New Orleans" that was to follow.

Men dressed as British and American soldiers came onto the field, cannons started exploding from all corners — a deafening noise. The horse that was carrying a man portraying Andrew Jackson went into a panic and nearly threw him and, contrary to the history books, the British were winning easily. The public-address announcer, supplementing the action below with historical facts, said, "When the smoke cleared, the British had lost 1,975 men while the American casualties were six killed and seven wounded." But below him the British were turning it into a rout, advancing at will. When it all ended, mercifully for many fans and the television audience, one could only wonder about the value of half-time and pregame shows. Besides wasting money, their most anticipated segments are the endings.

In the third period, the Chiefs, after listening to Hank Stram tell them, "Thirty minutes more and we're world champions. Play control ball," ate up five minutes with a drive after taking the kickoff. But a penalty stopped it and the Chiefs punted. Taking over on their own 31, the Vikings resembled the team from Minnesota for the first time. Kapp, mixing plays well, moved the ball to the Chiefs' 4-yard line in ten plays. Then Dave Osborn went over

Chief defenders, left to right, Buchanan, Culp, Mays and Bell.

Bill Brown found the going sticky against Jim Lynch and his mates.

his right tackle, Ron Yary, for the touchdown, and Fred Cox kicked the extra point, cutting it to 16–7 with well over a period and a half remaining.

But Kansas City, taking the kickoff, moved to the Vikings' 46 in five plays. Then Dawson threw a short pass to Otis Taylor, who started moving toward open field, but corner back Earsell Mackbee moved in and grabbed him. Taylor broke the tackle and continued on his way until running into safety Karl Kassulke at the 20. Giving Kassulke a slight fake to the inside, he went right over him, kicking his way into the end zone. It was a 46-yard play and, after another successful conversion by Stenerud, made the score 23–7, which would hold up to the end.

"It was only a six-yard B pass," said Taylor later. "I got hit on the left side and spun out. Then I hit the last guy downfield with my hand. I always try to punish a pass defender, just as he does me. I wanted to score that touchdown. I remembered watching Minnesota come back to beat the Rams and I felt we needed to keep scoring today."

"After that play," said Mackbee later, "my arm went numb and I didn't feel it anymore."

The game was over, except for the ticking. The only significant development that occurred after Taylor's touchdown came with four minutes left. The Chiefs, who had been confusing the Vikings with end-arounds and play-actions with such ease that one could only feel embarrassed for Minnesota for deluding itself into thinking it was ready to play this game, added one final humiliation. Aaron Brown put Kapp out of the game with a hard but clean tackle. Kapp had tried a bootleg play, hoping to go around Brown and Buck Buchanan. But Brown hit him violently behind the line of scrimmage and they both went down; only Brown got up. Kapp, holding his left shoulder, was helped off the field by his teammates. He slumped on the bench, a white towel covering his head, grimacing in pain. The injury was later diagnosed as a severe bruise.

But the American Football League, personified by the Chiefs on this day, had evened the score in Super Bowls at two games each. It would stay that way for infinity — it was the last Super Bowl game in which the American League would be represented. Hereafter, with the merger between the leagues, the AFL would be known as the American Conference of the National Football League.

Back in the locker room, the Chiefs' critiqued the victory in the usual abstract of football metaphors.

"We didn't put any new wrinkles in for this game," said Hank Stram. "The end-around surprised them, but it wasn't a new play. It might have been new to them, but we've used it before. Fortunately, it wasn't in the game films the Vikings had seen of us."

Otis Taylor high-steps his way to a scor

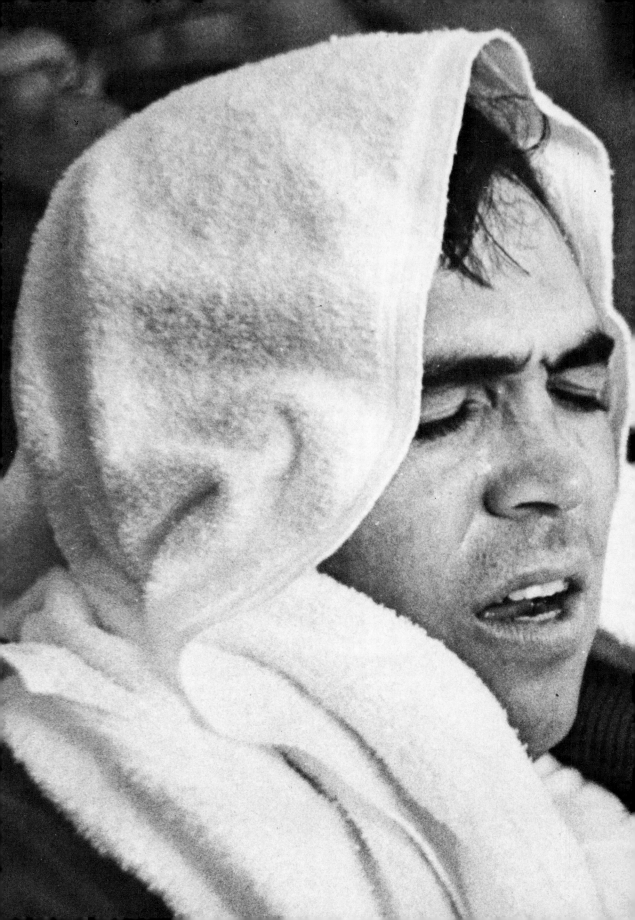

It is football tradition to cloud the obvious in the sublime. One could conclude that Stram was saying that the Vikings weren't as fully prepared for the Chiefs as they thought they were; but since he didn't say it in those words, it went unimplied in the next day's newsprint.

"We knew we could move the ball on them," said Ed Budde. "We stuck to the game plan and Lenny called it beautifully — traps, sweeps, screens, play-acts, passing. Dave Hill did an outstanding job on Carl Eller and so did Jim Tyrer on Jim Marshall."

(Translation: "The Vikings' front four was overrated and we knew it. Eller and Marshall just aren't that good.")

"We socked it to them," said Jerry Mays. "We felt if we could outhit them, we could beat them."

(Translation: "The Vikings thought they were physical. They let down after we started kicking hell out of them.")

"We knew that if we could take away their running game it would be a big factor," said Willie Lanier. "We used a tackle head-on with their center, either Buck Buchanan or Curley Culp, and it confused them."

(Translation: "The Vikings had no running game, and we proved it.")

As the corps of newsmen swarmed into the locker room, it seemed to head in one direction — Len Dawson's cubicle. But Dawson was occupied with Frank Gifford, the former New York Giant back turned sportscaster, who was conducting the postgame show for CBS. Gifford, it has been said, is a popular football announcer because he says nothing nicely. True to form, he asked Dawson about the game plan and the Vikings' defense; the pass to Otis Taylor and the end-arounds by Pitts; the running of Garrett and the blocking of Budde. But he did not ask him about the gambling report or the pressure he had been under. It was as if the shill in him suppressed whatever reporting instincts he might have had. Gifford, by side-stepping the most important question, confirmed his house-man's reputation for at least another year.

Mike Garrett, the effervescent running back, got up on the platform with Gifford after Dawson departed and did not give Gifford a chance to tie him up in rhetoric. Garrett said, "Just want to say I remember what Vince Lombardi said three years ago about us; that we're not as good as a lot of teams in the NFL." Then he looked up at the camera:

"Love ya, Vince."

Dawson came back to his locker, where the writers were waiting, and was asked about the gambling report.

"I don't think the victory vindicated anything," he said. "Unfortunately, the gambling report put a great deal of stress and strain on me, and more so on my family. But I asked the Good Lord to give me the strength and

137

For Joe Kapp it was a painful experience.

courage to play my best, and I asked him to let the sun shine on my team-mates today. I did have a lot of moral support in the form of letters and telegrams, thousands of them, from all over the country and especially from Kansas City.

"No, the gambling thing didn't give me any extra incentive. How could it? I approached this game as a big game, as an opportunity to be the best. You don't need any outside motivation. When you're on the field, your concentration is on the game and you do your job. I didn't give the gambling report a single thought out there."

(Translation: "It was on my mind, but I tried not to think about it.")

A man came by and informed Dawson that he had been selected as the game's Most Valuable Player and would receive a Dodge Charger from *Sport* magazine, an annual gift.

"Thank you," said Dawson, and he smiled for the first time.

In the Vikings' locker room, Joe Kapp sat on a trainer's table while a doctor looked at his injured left shoulder and suggested that he go immediately to a hospital for X-rays.

"Joe was writhing in pain earlier," said one of the Vikings. "He couldn't even talk. We had to wash him in the shower."

The Vikings, like all losers in football games, flattered the Chiefs, as if victory automatically merits accolades — "You've got to give Kansas City credit, that's all" (Carl Eller); "I felt we were aggressive enough on defense, but that didn't seem to bother the Chiefs" (Alan Page); "The Chiefs' defensive line is like a redwood forest in California" (Kapp); "We played a great team today, and it beat us" (Bud Grant).

Hubert Humphrey, former Senator from Minnesota, former Vice-President and unsuccessful Democratic candidate for President, came into the locker room and shook hands with the Viking players.

"Things just weren't clicking for us today," Humphrey said, and several of the players nodded automatically.

(Translation: "I've got nothing to say.")

In a small room adjacent to the Kansas City locker room, Len Dawson had a telephone receiver to his ear while newsmen with notebooks were hanging over his shoulders.

"D-A-W-S-O-N," he said twice to the long-distance operator, "Lenny Dawson."

There was a pause of nearly a minute, then Dawson broke the silence:

"Hello? Hello? Yes . . . Mister President."

The man on the other end, Richard Nixon, calling for the second time that day from the White House, said to him, "The world looks up to pro

Hank Stram at the summit.

football players for courage."

"Thank you, Mister President," answered Dawson, a finger in his right ear to keep out the surrounding noise. "We try to exemplify the good in professional football. . . . I appreciate it, Mister President. . . . But it wasn't me, sir; it was the whole team that did it."

Nixon also complimented Dawson on playing so well under such adverse conditions. The conversation lasted for six minutes, a call worth $2.68.

KANSAS CITY, Jan. 12 (AP) — The Kansas City Chiefs, conquerors of the Minnesota Vikings in the Super Bowl, today came home for a heroes' welcome.

Thousands jammed a parade route through the downtown streets and sirens blared as Kansas City hysterically celebrated its first world championship in any sport.

The Chiefs' chartered jet from New Orleans, scene of Kansas City's 23–7 upset victory over Minnesota of the National Football League yesterday, landed at Kansas City International Airport about 14 miles north of the downtown area. No one but airport personnel was permitted entry at the field.

(Today's homecoming was pre-arranged after thousands jammed the municipal airport terminal — tying up highway traffic and pouring onto the airport's runway — the night the Chiefs returned home after beating the Oakland Raiders for the AFL title.)

Police estimated that 100,000 people lined the parade route today. Ticker-tape and confetti poured from office buildings as the red and white convertibles carrying Coach Hank Stram and his players moved slowly to Liberty Memorial Mall, south of the city, where a ceremony was held. The governors of Missouri and Kansas proclaimed today as "Kansas City Chiefs Day" in both states.

NEW YORK, Jan. 12 (AP) — The Columbia Broadcasting System announced today that the Super Bowl football game yesterday between Kansas City and Minnesota at New Orleans attracted a television audience of about 60 million people. The network said ratings indicated that the game was watched on 23,050,000 television sets. It was, CBS said, the largest television audience ever to watch a single sports event.

LAS VEGAS, Jan. 12 (UPI) — Heavy bettors suffered substantial losses as a result of Kansas City's upset victory over Minnesota in the Super Bowl yesterday. Nevada's legal bookmakers were evasive, as usual, regarding the

Thank you, Mr. President.

amount of money wagered on either team. But it was understood generally that the two-point rise in the point spread favoring the Vikings during the week before the game indicated that large sums of money were lost on the NFL champions.

Minnesota had opened as an 11-point favorite on most books and, as money poured in on the Vikings, the "spot" rose steadily until it reached 13 points at game time.

The last-minute flurry of Kansas City money at 13 points by smaller bettors was reported to have cut down on the bookmakers' profits.

The day after the game, United Press International reported that additional information in the gambling investigation in Michigan had been uncovered.

A UPI dispatch said:

Four professional football quarterbacks, including Super Bowl hero Len Dawson, have received telephone calls from a big-time Detroit-area gambler, according to reports published today.

Besides Dawson, who led the Kansas City Chiefs to the world championship yesterday, Bill Munson of the Detroit Lions and Karl Sweetan of the Los Angeles Rams also received calls from Donald (Dice) Dawson (no relation to the quarterback), according to articles in *Time* and *Newsweek* magazines.

Newsweek also said Donald Dawson placed calls to the home of Joe Namath of the New York Jets, while *Time* included Frank Kush, head football coach at Arizona State University, among the persons receiving calls from the gambler.

Donald Dawson was one of 14 persons arrested by federal agents in a series of raids on New Year's Day. The raids were aimed at breaking what was called a national betting operation.

Time, which also revealed that Donald Dawson dined a number of times at the home of Jerome Cavanagh when Cavanagh was mayor of Detroit, said investigators could not learn what was said in any of Dawson's phone calls and all requests to tap the conversations were denied by the Justice Department's "top echelon."

Len Dawson, when his name cropped up in the investigation, admitted knowing Donald Dawson and both magazines quoted the quarterback as saying: "I have known Mr. Dawson for about 10 years. My only conversations with him in recent years concerned my knee injuries and the death of my father."

Newsweek said, "If there were any two things a gambler such as Donald Dawson would have wanted to know about a quarterback, of course, they would have been the condition of his knees and his feelings when his father died a few days before a big game."

Time concluded, "The condition of a quarterback's knees can be highly relevant in sports betting, but whether Donald Dawson qualified as a 'notorious character' is uncertain. Despite his reputation in Detroit, Donald Dawson's luck until this month was such that he had never even been arrested."

Len Dawson and the others named in Bill Matney's original report for NBC were never called to testify before the Federal Grand Jury. The case against Donald (Dice) Dawson was put in limbo. Many people in professional football dismissed Matney's report as being "much ado about nothing." But Matney saw it a different way.

"Nixon killed the whole investigation," he said. "By calling the Chiefs twice — before the game and after it to talk with Dawson himself — he virtually cleared Dawson and the others from any wrongdoing. How could the Justice Department continue to pursue the case when the President of the United States — its boss, literally — goes around calling prospective witnesses and tells them the world is looking up to them for courage? I'm not saying that Lenny Dawson did a single thing wrong. I'm not saying that Dawson knew any gamblers, socially or otherwise. I'm not saying that any of the other football players did either. I'm not saying anybody's guilty or not guilty.

"All I'm saying is that Nixon's phone calls to Stram and Dawson put the whole investigation on ice."

SUPER BOWL V

"I'M AN AQUARIUS"

Participants — Dallas Cowboys, champions of the National Football Conference, and Baltimore Colts, champions of the American Football Conference.

Date — January 17, 1971.

Site — Orange Bowl Stadium, Miami, Florida.

Time — 2:10 P.M., EDT.

Attendance — 80,577

Radio and Television — National Broadcasting Company (TV and Radio).

Regular-Season Records — Baltimore, 11-2-1; Dallas 10-4.

Playoff Records — Baltimore defeated Oakland Raiders, 27-17, for AFC title; Dallas defeated San Francisco 49ers, 17-10, for NFC title.

Players' Shares — $15,000 to each member of winning team; $7,500 to each member of losing team.

Gate Receipts — Estimated $800,000.

Radio-TV Receipts — $2,750,000.

Officials — Referee, Norm Schachter; Umpire, Paul Trepinski; Head Linesman, Ed Marion; Line Judge, Jack Fette; Field Judge, Fritz Graf; Back Judge, Hugh Gamber.

Coaches — Don McCafferty, Baltimore; Tom Landry, Dallas.

BALTIMORE, Jan. 7 (UPI) — The Baltimore Colts, trying to forget their last disastrous trip to the Super Bowl, are doing everything differently this year.

The Colts worked out today in sub-freezing weather for the final time, then flew to Miami to continue drills for their Jan. 17 game against the Dallas Cowboys.

The Colts went south on a different airline (Eastern instead of United), and they will be lodged at a different site (The Miami Lakes Country Club instead of the Statler-Hilton Hotel), and they will practice on a different field (Biscayne College instead of St. Andrew's Boys School in Boca Raton) than they did in 1969 when they lost to the New York Jets in Super Bowl III.

"'Ego,'" wrote Norman Mailer, "is the great word of the 20th Century. If there is a single word our century has added to the potentiality of language, it is 'ego.' Everything we have done in this century, from monumental feats to nightmares of human destruction, has been a function of that extraordinary state of the psyche which gives us the authority to declare we are sure of ourselves when we are not. Yes, ego — that officious and sometimes efficient exercise of ignorance-as-authority — must be the central phenomenon of the 20th Century, even if patriotic Americans like to pretend it does not exist in their heroes. Which, of course, is part of the holy American horseball."

One remembers the Baltimore Colts swaggering out of Municipal Stadium in Cleveland on a dark, cold Sunday afternoon in December, 1968,

146

after defeating the Cleveland Browns, 34–0, in the NFL championship game, vainglorious in their smugness, pretending to be something more than mortal; a defensive team with no peer in the history of the game, a team that was one victory from being recognized, perhaps, as the best ever to play in a football game. But two weeks later the Baltimore Colts were hanging their heads as they left the Orange Bowl in Miami, their collective egos reduced to the scrambled-eggs-on-concrete of men who had reached bottom after falls from windows twenty stories high. The New York Jets, who defeated the Colts that day, 16–7, destroyed not only a myth of invincibility but lanced the festering boil of Baltimore arrogance and drained it over the accomplishments of an entire Colt season.

Many things happened to the Baltimore Colts after that game in January, 1969. They sleepwalked through a lackluster 1969 season; their owner, Carroll Rosenbloom, in exchange for three million dollars, put them in the American Conference of the National Football League, a move that helped cement the merger of the leagues; Don Shula, their coach, respected as a tactician but never popular among his players, left to become head coach of the Miami Dolphins; Rosenbloom, incensed, accused the Dolphins of tampering illegally with his hired help, pressed the issue to the commissioner's office and wound up with a Miami draft choice as compensation.

When Shula left, Bubba Smith, one of pro football's better defensive ends, was hardly overcome with remorse. Smith said, "Fine, maybe we'll get a coach now who'll treat us like human beings instead of dogs." John Mackey, the tight end, said that if coaches could break contracts with their teams and presumably better their stations in life with jobs that paid more money, then players should have the same opportunity. As president of the players' association, he put the issue into his plank for players' liberation, so to speak, and wound up as the leader of a players' strike in July and August, 1970, that threatened to wipe out the entire season. Shula, it was clear, did not depart to the accompaniment of tinkling champagne glasses; more the sound of flying beer cans.

With Shula gone, the dormant egos of the Colts seemed to squirm for feeding again. Like hatched robins, mouths agape, they waited for the first worm. His replacement, Don McCafferty, formerly a Colt assistant, was the antithesis of Shula, a warm, potbellied stove as opposed to a whistling tea kettle. McCafferty soothed the clipped wings by massaging them with salve and did not threaten budding individuality with extensive game plans or the personal demeanor of Napoleon possessed, returning from Elba. Still, through most of the 1970 season, the Colts were more stagger than swagger. They did not roll through the American Conference like a threshing machine, leaving pretzeled bodies in their path. They barely won games in which they were heavily favored, resembling overworked tractors. Their spirits

147

received a dose of whipped cream when they defeated the New York Jets in October, a game in which their nemesis, Joe Namath, broke a bone in his throwing hand and was left idle for the rest of the season. Finally, they won playoff games by seventeen and ten points and came into the Super Bowl game willing, if not eager, to put their reconstructed egos on the line for the first time in two years.

Mike Curtis, the Baltimore linebacker who flaunts the nickname "The Animal," was among the twenty-four Colt players who ran the gantlet from January, 1969. He said, after arriving in Miami:

"My God, no one knows the despair, the abject humiliation, we felt that day. The 1968 Baltimore Colts, a perfect football machine. The 1968 Baltimore Colts, who crushed every opponent but one on a tough schedule. The 1968 Baltimore Colts . . . the first National Football League team to lose the Super Bowl.

"I felt great anger inside of me that day. Those damn Jets, for one thing, were holding as if they were never going to hold again. They haven't stopped yet. The worst offender of all, Winston Hill, makes All-AFL. But even worse, I hate guys who steal a pass and then stuff it in the victim's face, humiliating him. It's cheap and it's miserable, the act of an incompetent and a loudmouth, and Johnny Sample is a perfect example of both.

"Going into that game, we heard over and over again that we've got to beat that longhair. Yeah, I thought, we've got to beat that longhair. But there was no dishonor in losing to the best — and that's what Namath was. But losing to the Samples and the Hills . . . man, that was degrading."

So, as the Colts arrived in Miami to prepare for their second Super Bowl game, they were being motivated by two factors: 1) Vindicating themselves for the loss to the Jets in 1969, and 2) proving to pro football that they could win games without the coaching of Don Shula. Still, the very presence of the Colts in this Super Bowl eliminated the most desirable ingredient — a representative of the old American Football League. No matter how hard the energetic young men in Pete Rozelle's office attempted to camouflage the Colts' presence, the team *was not* a member of the old AFL; it *did not* have the moral backing of the other teams in the AFL, most of which were charter AFL clubs. And even more significant, perhaps, the Colts *did not* regard themselves as representatives of anything more expansive than Chesapeake Bay.

"I don't want to win one for the old AFC," said Billy Ray Smith, the seasoned defensive tackle. "I want to win one for old B.R. and the Colts. This will be my last game . . . unless I turn referee. Why shouldn't I feel that way? We've been in the AFC for one season — how in hell can the league identify with us, and vice-versa? We're still the Colts the Jets beat to a lot of people in the league. Nobody's sending us telegrams this year."

Don McCafferty took over the reins of the Colts with a quiet certainty.

Although he missed the Colts by over a half-century, H. L. Mencken, one of Baltimore's more caustic citizens at a time when the city's only colts were young horses, might have written about Baltimore's appearance in this game in the following manner:

"The sheer stupidity of the American masses has never been more evident than in this folly masquerading as a game between the two best professional football teams on the face of the earth. For the masses to swallow the Baltimore team's designation as 'Champion of the American Football Conference' is incredible; but that species of boobus Americanus continually outdoes itself on the most minuscule of issues. Only fools would spend money to see this game, believing it is a pure and true matchup of the two best teams in each conference. The truth of the matter is that the game should be canceled because of the hypocrisy of the matchup, and pro football investigated for allowing such a debacle to come about. But the fools pay anyway, descending upon Miami like mad lemmings to the sea; wasn't it just two years ago that these same gullible minds were chastising the Baltimore Colts for losing to the American League? Now the Baltimore Colts are Americans themselves; was that the penalty they suffered for losing that game to the New York Jets? Or is it I who have the jaded view, believing, as I do, that once the labels and the categories are stripped away, the Baltimore Colts are still the same old Baltimore Colts — and what the hell are they doing in this game?"

> MIAMI, Jan. 9 (AP) — The Super Bowl game has been sold out for weeks — long before the tickets went on public sale. All 79,000 available seats in the Orange Bowl are gone for the game between Baltimore and Dallas. Scalpers in this area are already rubbing their hands in anticipation.

The Dallas Cowboys, arriving a week before the game at their lodging and training sites in Fort Lauderdale, had a stigma about them that bordered on sorcery. Whereas the Colts had bumbled only one big game, the Cowboys had bumbled many, mysteriously and without logical explanation. The Colts of 1969 and Tom Dewey of 1948 did it only once, but the Cowboys seemed to be continuously snatching defeat from the jaws of victory.

Talent the Cowboys did not lack — in fact, they had an abundance of it. Their special teams were the best in the game; the players who were running down punt-returners and plunging headlong into the meatgrinder of defensive wedges would have been starters at regular positions on other teams. The enigma of the Cowboys, it seemed, was their lack of passion, a problem that traced to their head coach, Tom Landry. A student of football technology as Wernher von Braun is a student of aerospace technology, Landry sometimes could not see his players for his programs. Although he

150

Mike (The Animal) Curtis had known humiliation and despair.

served his pro apprenticeship alongside Vince Lombardi (they were both assistant coaches for the New York Giants), he never beat Lombardi in a stakes game, although the differences in the strengths of their teams were microscopic most of the time.

But Lombardi used passion to arouse and motivate his Green Bay Packers and Landry used computerized cards and a dialect that seemed borrowed from the NASA Space Center in Houston. When Dallas lost its second straight NFL playoff game to the Cleveland Browns in 1969, Landry promised to give the Cowboys a "top-to-bottom scientific re-evaluation," which prompted a battery of motivation tests and a bevy of data cards on player performance levels. One could envision Lombardi approaching the same problem by promising each of his players hard kicks in soft places.

Landry started the 1970 season by benching his wide receiver, Bob Hayes, for failing to live up to his performance level. Then he alternated Roger Staubach and Craig Morton at quarterback, calling the plays for both on the sidelines. Calvin Hill, an outstanding running back, injured his leg and was replaced by a rookie, Duane Thomas. By midseason, in a Monday night television game against the St. Louis Cardinals, the Cowboys looked so languid in losing, 38–0, that even their former quarterback, Don Meredith, in the broadcasting booth, disowned them. "This ain't the Cowboy team I used to know," he said, his twang twisted by embarrassment and rage. Then, a few weeks later, split end Lance Rentzel was arrested in Dallas on a charge of exposing himself to a ten-year-old girl and went into voluntary retirement. Rumors were becoming persistent, too, that some of the Cowboy players were deep into the drug scene — marijuana and heroin, not just greenies and pain-killers — as Ira Berkow reported for Newspaper Enterprise Association. On November 16, after the loss to St. Louis, the Cowboys had a 5–4 record and seemed on the verge of joining the ranchowner on the Pedernales in oblivion.

But the defensive unit, as if realizing at last that the team's success or failure rested squarely upon it, suddenly turned itself into the best in the game for the last half of the season. The offense, meanwhile, scored just enough to win — the Cowboys beat Detroit, 5–0, and San Francisco, 17–10, in playoff games — and Morton, the quarterback, seemed to be a marionette on the brink of coming to life, calling audibles at the line with the audacity of a Joe Namath. Duane Thomas, the rookie running back, was doing so well that he kept Calvin Hill, healed by now, on the bench, and Hayes, reinserted into the lineup sans IBM cards, was not only making some of the most spectacular plays of his career but was actually spotted blocking for his backs on occasion.

But the 1970 season could not be described as a rewarding one for the Dallas Cowboys; they became winners only when faced with the prospect of

153

Duane Thomas was the Cowboys' big running threat.

humiliation. That they did succeed in a 180-degree turnabout indicated a great deal of pluckiness, if not damned, dogged determination. But there remained something suspect about this team that had its coach calling all the plays from the sidelines, a practice that camouflaged his lack of confidence in his quarterback with the implication that he was taking the pressure off of him. Morton, however, regardless of whatever inner repulsion he must have harbored, accepted the practice as dutifully as writers accept nitpicking editors.

Robert F. Jones, in Sports Illustrated, *wrote of Morton:*

> There is this one slow, sad truth about pro quarterbacks: Almost to a man they are deadly dull. It is as if the game they dominate, with its brute violence and constant pain, has leeched them of precisely those qualities — fury, rage, sharpness of tongue — that make other, lesser men appear more interesting. For every Joe Namath or Joe Kapp, there are five Bart Starrs, so clean and straight and self-effacing that they make one yearn, say, for the ribald companionship of St. Francis of Assisi. As the Cowboys prepared for their first Super Bowl game, Craig Morton's already legendary reputation for deathless dialogue took a new turn. He developed laryngitis. Forbidden by his doctor to speak for two days, and afterward in a whisper, Morton kept to his Playboy-modern apartment, attended only by a game plan, a girl named Patty and the sounds of silence.

But Morton finally outdid himself later when he responded to a question about what turned the Cowboys around.

"The Cleveland game was the one," he whispered. "We had a way of going under against those guys when something went against us. In the Browns game, when Bobby Hayes dropped a punt for a safety, we began to get together. Before, we might have caved in with a bad break. Well, here it comes again. Fate, you know. But everyone sort of said, 'That's okay, Bobby. We'll get it back.' And we did and we won and we kept on winning. I really can't explain why; we just did, that's all."

From News Dispatches of January 11:

Tickets to the Super Bowl football game in Miami's Orange Bowl are as scarce as tickets to a Presidential Inaugural Ball.

"There is no doubt that ticket pressure is mounting," said Jim Kensil, assistant commissioner of the National Football League. "There are a dozen ways in which to get Super Bowl tickets, but people have got to act fast before the supply evaporates."

Season-ticket holders of the Miami Dolphins scooped up the largest batch, about 25,000. They are allowed to buy them on a one-for-one basis

155

Craig Morton didn't do much talking before the game.

for their regular-season commitments.

The Colts and the Cowboys receive team allotments of ten thousand tickets each. The twenty-four remaining NFL franchises are allotted five hundred each. The news media are allowed to purchase one thousand. Persons with the right political connections are allocated another thousand. The remaining tickets are split among NFL officials, television and radio sponsors, NFL players and participants in the game, such as members of the marching bands.

This year, the NFL office said, tickets for the end zone sold faster at fifteen dollars each than they had three years ago at six dollars each.

There are only one thousand no-strings-attached tickets sold for the "little guy," who can line up and buy space without the right political or team connections. They were sold in a very few minutes one Sunday afternoon in November at an Orange Bowl ticket window.

On Wednesday the Colts returned from a practice session at Biscayne College and lounged on the premises of the Miami Lakes Country Club — a spot so secluded that the nearest form of life was a residential section of expensive Tudor and Colonial homes a mile or so away.

John Mackey, the tight end who was president of the players' association and leader of a strike that curtailed training camps and nearly canceled the entire 1970 season, was asked by a reporter if the situation between players and owners had improved any?

"Yes and no," said Mackey. "Some things have been solved and some things haven't. In two weeks, after the Pro Bowl in Los Angeles, we'll have a meeting and decide where we're going. But nobody is bothering me now about labor things. I've got a game to get ready for. All the players have been pretty considerate, they've been leaving me alone. They know I'll be available to them on Sunday night if anything comes up.

"The big obstacle before us is whether or not to include coaches in the players' pension plan. Our contract on the issue hasn't been signed yet. In the confusion of getting a settlement last summer, some misunderstanding developed about it. But I really can't talk about it now. I've got to think about playing Dallas."

The reporter asked Mackey just how much the loss to the Jets in 1969 was motivating the Colts in 1971?

"I think of sitting around at half time of that game two years ago, and how bad it was, how unprepared we were. And funny, I remember that the night before that game was the only time my wife has ever stayed with me before a game. No, I'm not blaming the loss on her — it's just something I remember, that's all.

"I dropped a few passes in that game, but I'm not haunted by them.

Those things just happen. On one pass, I lost it in the background of the spectators. It's hard to see in this stadium because of the colorful crowd. All the people in different clothes — orange, red, green, white, you name it.

"But I was low, man, real low, after that game. I was low for five, six months. I remember feeling like I wanted to dig a hole and hide until the next season started.

"This year, everybody's been knocking us. But we got better as the season went on. We had some new players, we were in a new league and we had new defensive alignments to face. It was an adjustment for the veterans as well as the rookies. Early in the year we had to do a lot of thinking about things.

"Now we don't have to think at all."

From News Dispatches of January 12:

The Dallas Cowboys began their final series of practices today for Sunday's Super Bowl game, and Calvin Hill, all but forgotten the last two months, was back in the spotlight. Hill, the NFL's Rookie of the Year in 1969, was running in the first backfield with the 1970 rookie who took his job away, Duane Thomas.

With Hill at halfback, Thomas moved over a couple steps to the fullback spot, filling in for the injured Walt Garrison, the regular who worked out gingerly under sunny skies in eighty-degree temperatures. Garrison caught the touchdown pass that beat San Francisco in the NFL championship game but came out of that contest with a badly twisted ankle to go along with his previously strained knee and chipped collarbone.

Later in the day, Coach Tom Landry and his staff gave the players their offensive game plan in a forty-five-page blue notebook. Because the Baltimore defenses are so varied in appearance, Landry and his staff felt they needed a full repertoire. But once the game begins, Landry, who calls all the plays from the sidelines, will be eliminating them by the handful.

"You find out quickly what is going to work against their defenses," said Jim Myers, an assistant offensive coach, "and then you throw out what won't work. The process of elimination. When you settle on what is going to work, you keep repeating it. That's the big factor, to repeat and repeat and repeat."

Bob Hayes, the Dallas wide receiver, sitting on a lounge chair near the pool of the Cowboys' motel, was asked by a reporter if he remembered mounting the victory stand in the 1964 Olympic Games in Tokyo wearing a cowboy hat? Hayes said that he did.

"What ever made you wear that hat?" the reporter pressed.

"Tell you the truth," said Hayes, "I was so excited about getting the

157

gold medal, I forgot I was wearing the thing."

The cowboy hats were the idea of a United States Olympic Committee official who thought they would bring a touch of the Wild West of old America to the Orient. Most of the American athletes refused to wear the hats, claiming they looked hideous and demeaning, and buried them deep in their closets. Hayes said he was embarrassed by the hat once he had realized that it did not exactly blend in with a blue sweatsuit and gold medal.

During that Olympiad, Hayes set a world record in the one-hundred-yard dash with a time of ten seconds flat. But he was even faster running the anchor one-hundred-meter leg in the four-hundred-meter relay. The first three Americans were less than exceptional in that race; in fact, Hayes took off in sixth place, four yards behind Jocelyn Delecour of France. But in the straightaway, Hayes passed one runner after another until he crossed the finish line with an astounding lead of three yards.

Rut Walker, an American track coach, looked at his stopwatch and said, "This is ridiculous. I just timed Hayes in 8.6 seconds."

"Of course it's ridiculous," said Bob Giegengack, the head coach. "But if you told me he just ran the anchor in nothing flat I'd believe you."

Hayes joined the Cowboys the following year and was unchallenged as the fastest wide receiver in football. But the 1970 season was a strange one for him. When Landry, the Dallas coach, benched him for not playing up to his performance potential, the move stunned not only Hayes himself but most football fans. For five seasons, Hayes' presence alone had made opposing defenses change their personalities.

But the Hayes-Landry episode seemed to be another example of the continuing gap between middle-aged white coaches and young black athletes. Coaches, accustomed to the gung-ho-raw-meat effervescence of white players who enjoy contact, hold them up as model performers. As the game's celebrated dropout, Dave Meggyesy, said, coaches interpret that effervescence as being a trait in making the player "coachable." Yet a whole new breed of black players, with icicle exteriors, marching to the beat of their own distant drummers, performed their duties better than most of the model white players without any of the coach-pleasing excitement. Coaches felt that the lack of surface enthusiasm denoted laziness. It was a situation not common in football alone — Richie Allen said the Philadelphia Phillies treated him like an animal when he was injured because they felt black players were forever dogging it; Reggie Jackson said the Oakland A's management overreacted to his batting slump because it was frustrated by its own lack of knowledge in dealing with the black psyche. The best example, of course, was Muhammad Ali, who sent white, middle-age boxing fans to their barrooms shaking their heads in their boilermakers because he was a heavyweight champion who didn't want to be hit — and won his first

Olympic champion Bob Hayes wore a cowboy hat long before he became a Cowboy.

twenty-nine fights anyway.

Whatever the reason, Hayes was disappointed in Landry's action, which was construed by some as being the coach's way of shaking up the team. Landry, in explaining the move, said, "Bob just wasn't meeting the requirements for what an end does or should do." But by the ninth game, after Hayes was reinserted in the lineup, Landry's evaluation had changed. "The Thanksgiving Day game against Green Bay," said Landry, "was the best game I've ever seen Bob Hayes play."

True to form, Hayes accepted the compliment with all the jubilation of a man waiting for the trapdoor to be sprung.

"In that game," he said, "I went to throw a block at a linebacker. Suddenly, who's in front of me but Mike McCoy, all 280 pounds of him. He wiped me out, man; he wiped me out."

Charlie Waters, a rookie defensive safety for the Cowboys, told a reporter, "You know, a year ago this time I was sitting in a frat house at Clemson, watching the Super Bowl game on television. I had just had shoulder surgery. I was so convinced something like this was out of my reach that I didn't even bother to dream about it."

From News Dispatches of January 13:

A lawsuit aiming to lift the television blackout in the Miami area of the Super Bowl game on Sunday was dismissed today. It was filed by a local lawyer, Ellis Rubin. He reasoned that since the game was sold out, the 2.5 million owners of television sets in the Miami area deserved to see the game, especially since the City of Miami was spending tax money to stage it in the city-owned Orange Bowl.

A circuit court judge, Raymond Nathan, said that his court had no authority to lift the blackout and refused to issue an injunction. The National Football League has determinedly fought the case, another in the long line of challenges to pro football's policy of blacking out areas within a seventy-five-mile radius of games.

If there was one man who was held up above all the rest by most Americans as the epitome of what a professional football player was supposed to represent as a performer and a person, it was John Unitas. The quarterback of the Colts had spanned nearly a decade and a half as the measuring stick for all prospective quarterbacks (even Joe Namath wore No. 19 in high school in emulation of Unitas), and his demeanor as a person was exemplary. He was, in the eyes of much of America, the model citizen — family man, businessman, team man without flaw.

But going into this Super Bowl game, John Unitas was carrying an

161

Dallas coach Tom Landry couldn't please everybody all the time.

extra burden of personal problems, but he did not give the impression that something was troubling him during his meetings with the press.

"When we first got to Miami," said Ernie Accorsi, the Colts' public relations director, "I had a long talk with John. I told him that the place is going to be crawling with media people and ninety percent of them are going to want to talk with him. I suggested that in order to make it easy for him we stage two press conferences for him, lasting about an hour each, and let the press fire away. The rest of the time we'd keep everybody away from him. He said fine, it was a good idea.

"John was like a real pro both times. He was right on time and answered questions politely and at length, and everybody was satisfied. He didn't say anything that bordered on controversy and, at times, he actually seemed to be enjoying the sessions. The newspaper guys were happy and, as usual, John got most of the space.

"There were other things on his mind, sure, but this wasn't the time or the place to discuss them. Very few people were aware of the situation that was bothering John, and John sure as hell wasn't going to go around volunteering things."

Unitas' wife, Dorothy, would later file suit for divorce, charging him with adultery.

When he joined the Colts from Michigan State University, Charles (Bubba) Smith was immediately ordained as the best young defensive end in the game. Cries of "Kill, Bubba, Kill" came drifting down from the rafters of Memorial Stadium in Baltimore and, when he did get his hand on an opposing quarterback, he fed the fantasies by grinding the passer into the dirt.

But Don Shula, among others, detected a flaw in the demeanor of early Bubba Smith — he did not rush hard on every play. There were times when it appeared that Bubba Smith was resting when he should have been rushing, and there were occasions when Shula criticized him for it. Bubba Smith resented the implication, not to mention the criticism.

"Any time you're not there clawing away at quarterbacks, people think you're not comin'," he said. "The longest day I've ever spent on a football field was against the Jets in New York this season. Namath threw sixty-two passes that day and I know I was rushing hard on every damn one of them. It got so that the Jets were using two, three guys to block me.

"When Shula was here, he'd get upset about a lot of things and start hollering. Shula is exceptionally smart, and I'm not rapping him. I'd be the first to admit that he's brilliant. But I don't like to be hollered at. When my father coached me in high school, he kept a board with him and he'd whack me with it, but he didn't holler.

John Unitas was getting a second chance in the Super Bowl.

"McCafferty is beautiful, man. He doesn't holler at all. He's human, too. The other night he sat in on a poker game the guys were having. Shula never did anything like that. McCafferty sits right down, wins a fifty-dollar pot and then leaves. Beautiful, man. As a coach he's never tried to fool us about anything. He just lays it on the line. He hasn't got any set way, and everybody on this team will go out and break his neck for the guy."

Bob Asher, a Dallas rookie offensive tackle from Vanderbilt, was talking to a reporter about the influx of media people at the Cowboys' training site in Fort Lauderdale.

"Never seen so many writers around in my life," he said. "Tell you the truth, I'm getting tired of answering the same question, over and over."

"What question is that?" the reporter said.

Asher paused for a few seconds, then answered, "What's your name?"

> *MIAMI, Jan. 14 (AP) — For the first time in 69 years, fans of the victorious Rose Bowl team didn't tear down the goalposts in Pasadena. The goalpost makers were too slick for the fans.*
>
> *"I just couldn't afford it," said Joel Rottman, inventor of the single-standard goalposts. "If the posts had gone down, it would have cost me $1,775."*
>
> *Rottman holds a patent on the single-standard post now used by more than 300 pro, college and high school athletic fields. He sells the aluminum models for $1,775 a set, the steel models for $995.*
>
> *Rottman wanted to get his product into the Rose Bowl and finally made a sale—with unusual conditions— prior to the Jan. 1 game between Stanford and Ohio State. "The Rose Bowl people said fans always rip the goalposts down," said Rottman. "So they figured spending $1,775 was a bad investment. They said that the wooden ones would do."*
>
> *Rottman finally promised that if the fans ripped down his posts, the purchase price would be refunded in full. Then came the slick part.*
>
> *"We coated the posts with STP, the motor oil additive," he said. "It's clear and it's slick. Those Stanford fans tried their best, but found that it was like catching a greased pig. They finally gave up."*
>
> *Rottman's single-standard posts have been installed for the fifth Super Bowl game in the Orange Bowl Sunday.*

From News Dispatches of January 14:

Unlike two years ago, when cabdrivers were saying, "What football game? All the people down here care about is the horses," the City of Miami is excited, superficially at least, about the Super Bowl game.

It might have been the Jets' upset of the Colts here two years ago that turned them on, or it might have been the year's absence, with the game switching to New Orleans in 1970, that did it. Some people might even find the match between Baltimore and Dallas irresistible, although that seems questionable.

Whatever it is, this Super Bowl has generated a rare demand for tickets and even anticipation and excitement in this blasé city. The opening of Hialeah on Saturday, an annual occasion of note here, has been obscured by the game. The enlarged Orange Bowl has eighty thousand seats and they are all gone at fifteen dollars each.

"The ticket demand is still cresting," said Don Weiss, the NFL public relations director. "We could have sold 100,000 tickets for this game if we had the room."

John Niland, the Cowboys' offensive guard, had let a personal secret out earlier in the season — he was contributing one thousand dollars a year to his old high school in Amityville, Long Island, for what the school designated "The John Niland Scholarship."

"I was an orphan," said Niland, "and I grew up in poverty, although I didn't know it at the time. Amityville is in Suffolk County and some parts of it are pretty affluent. But I grew up on the wrong side of the tracks. It was called an industrial park and my house was right next door to a milk company and a truck company. I had my share of gang fights and street fights.

"We didn't have anything in the house — not even heat. But I didn't know the difference, I thought a lot of people lived the same way. I've always worked. I had my first job at ten or eleven, pumping gas at night. They paid me fifty cents a night and one free pizza pie.

"My adopted mother was fifty when she got me, and I was the only child. I was big for my age and played football in high school and did pretty well. But I had no idea of going to college. There was no money. I got some scholarship offers, one from Notre Dame and one from Syracuse and one from Iowa. I chose Iowa because the people there seemed interested in helping me as a person. They did, too, and I enjoyed it there. I really loved Iowa City.

"Now I make thirty thousand dollars a year playing football and close to thirty thousand more as a goodwill representative for a UHF television station and a savings bank. And each year I send a thousand dollars back to my old high school so it can help start some other athlete off in college. The money comes from fees I get as a dinner speaker. I make a lot of talks to kids' groups, and it's very important that I do. I certainly wish I had a

165

Sam Huff or a Rosey Brown coming around to talk to me when I was young.

"A lot of athletes have no idea how important they are as heroes to young people."

On Friday, at 1 A.M., in the Cafe Cristal in the Diplomat Hotel in Miami, Joey Heatherton began her last show of the night. Wearing a tight, strapless, full-length white gown, the spotlight blue, she oozed out the words to "It Had To Be You" as assuredly and seductively as if she had written them herself on a lonely night:

> *. . . I wandered around and finally found somebody who —*
> *Could make me be true, could make me be blue*
> *And even be glad, just to be sad, thinking of you. . . .*

Lance Rentzel stood in the rear of the lounge, watching his wife perform. Wearing a blue-striped shirt, black bow tie and black suit, he said that he had lost some weight in recent weeks and that he had been spending his time traveling with Joey because, "I don't have much else to do these days."

Joey's mid-January booking in the Diplomat Hotel was planned months in advance to coincide with the Super Bowl and the influx of football fans it would attract with time and money on their hands. That the Cowboys made it to the Super Bowl themselves was an unanticipated bonus. When the booking was made it was agreed that it would be a profitable arrangement no matter who played in the game; there would be many acquaintances of Joey and Lance in town who would stop by and have a drink or two and catch a couple of Joey's numbers before moving on to the next nightspot.

After the last show ended, Rentzel went backstage to congratulate Joey on her performance and ask after her, as she had been fighting off the flu. Soon he came out and talked to a friend and to Ira Berkow of NEA. He told Berkow that he had had little contact with his Cowboy teammates since he decided to voluntarily retire from football, although he had thought "a thousand times" about rejoining the club.

"There comes a time when you have to think of somebody other than yourself," he said. "It would have been unfair to subject the team to all the suffering I was going through."

He said he had given Bob Hayes a call, though — "Bob's my best friend on the team. I just wanted to know what was going on." He paused for a few seconds, then added, "I've had a lot of time to be by myself. In adversity you learn a lot about yourself. One thing I've learned is to appreciate what I've got. I've got a wife I love and appreciate and enjoy being with. And I've learned to appreciate what talents I do have."

166

At the Miami Lakes Country Club, forty-eight hours before the game, Roy Jefferson, the Colts' wide receiver, was talking about his old team, the Pittsburgh Steelers, who had traded him to Baltimore before the season started.

"The Steelers considered me good riddance," he said. "They felt they couldn't control me. They felt I was a menace to the team's morale. They felt I might alienate the players against the coaches. I was the team player representative. Maybe that influenced them, I don't know for sure.

"Chuck Noll, the coach, he said to me, 'You haven't reached your potential yet and I don't think you ever will.' But I believe he was really covering up some other reason. I still feel that I'm improving as a wide receiver.

"When we beat Oakland two weeks ago, I was the happiest guy in the dressing room. I made the most noise. I never had too many chances to celebrate in Pittsburgh. But I especially wanted to win that game because the Raiders were cocky. They brought all their equipment and their clothes for the two weeks between that game and this one. They were all set to come down here for the Super Bowl game.

"But — ha! — we're here instead."

Jim O'Brien, the Colts' rookie place-kicker, possessor of long sideburns and flowing locks that are growing into a mane down the back of his neck — a rarity among the Colts — talked about his days as a cadet at the Air Force Academy in Colorado Springs, Colorado.

"I hated it there," he said. "They recruited me pretty good and what does a kid from Cincinnati know? I lasted six months. I developed ulcers and left. I still feel the ulcers kick up once in a while. But the big reason was that I didn't like someone else telling me what to do. Not that I resent authority. It's just that there was so much Mickey Mouse stuff. I guess you can say that I'm just not shaped for the military world."

Another Colt rookie, Jack Maitland, a running back, was six months removed from Williams College in Williamstown, Massachusetts, a picturesque community in the Berkshire Mountains where the autumn foliage attracts more people than Williams' football games.

"I guess it's pretty unusual to go from a school like Williams to the Super Bowl," he said. "I'd have never believed it if it didn't happen. At Williams I played in the Little Three Conference. The other two schools were Amherst and Wesleyan. We usually had pretty good teams up there, but the atmosphere was a lot different than the atmosphere, say, at Ohio State.

"Up to this point I'd have to say my biggest thrill in football was making All-Little Three three years in a row."

167

Earl Morrall, the Colts' substitute quarterback again since John Unitas' shoulder had healed, was asked if he had any lingering effects from his dismal performance in the third Super Bowl game that led to the Colts' loss to the New York Jets?

"That was the biggest game of my life," he said, "and it didn't turn out too well. I've tried to shrug it off, but I just can't. I keep thinking about it and I still get flashbacks, remembering all the bad things and all of the turning points.

"I've replayed in my mind that whole game over and over again. The interceptions, the flea-flicker, the whole mess. Now that I'm back at the Super Bowl, I'll be returning to the scene of the crime. I guess there is no way I can escape it."

That night, in a Miami restaurant, Norman Schachter, a principal of a high school in Los Angeles and an NFL game official for seventeen years, assembled his six-man crew for a working dinner. Schachter, as referee, would be the game official in charge of the Super Bowl. His associates included Paul Trepinski, umpire; Ed Marion, head linesman; Jack Fette, line judge; Fritz Graf, field judge, and Hugh Gamber, back judge. The alternates, in case of emergency, were Jack Eader and Pat Harder.

Since the crew would be working together for the first time — three were from the American Conference and three from the National — Schachter gave them a briefing over dinner, the first of several that would continue through early morning on the day of the Super Bowl itself.

A rookie official makes $250 a game during the regular season. Those with tenure of eleven years or more make $500 a game. Usually, postseason games and league championships are scaled to between $700 and $1,000 a game. But for the Super Bowl game, Schachter and his crew would be paid $1,500 each.

The Saturday before the game was a quiet one as compared with the days before the two previous Super Bowls. Tom Landry, coach of the Cowboys, and Pete Rozelle, commissioner of pro football, had held press conferences in the Americana Hotel on Friday and their words took up most of the space in the sports pages of Saturday's newspapers.

Landry said that he was going to start Walt Garrison at fullback, despite all his injuries. Garrison, a steer wrestler in Texas rodeos in the off-season, had been a starter all season.

"Garrison has been improving each day," said Landry. "Right now he's seventy-five percent of himself, but by game time we feel he should be close to one hundred percent. We're going to go with him. He has been limping, but when he has the ball under his arm, he runs hard."

169

Colt rookie Jim O'Brien wasn't cut out for the wild blue yonder.

Rozelle, in his meeting with the press, touched upon a variety of subjects. He admitted that the lack of a representative of the old American Football League had detracted somewhat from the attraction, but was quick to point out that tickets had sold faster for this Super Bowl game than for any of the previous four.

But Rozelle's silver lining could not diminish the prospect of these two less-than-spectacular teams plowing through the trenches in a dull, unexciting game, the bland leading the bland. Jimmy (The Greek) Snyder, two-for-four in picking Super Bowls, installed Dallas as a one-point favorite in Las Vegas. Rozelle himself said that he was hoping the game ended in a tie, forcing a sudden-death overtime. But others were saying it was just another NFL championship game, with fancy trappings.

From News Dispatches of January 16:

Hialeah Race Track opened its forty-day meeting in perfect weather and drew a near-record crowd that established an opening-day betting record. Lion Sleeps, winner of four in a row at Tropical Park, which closed yesterday, led every step of the way to win the feature race, the $31,250 Super Bowl Handicap.

With Bobby Ussery up, Lion Sleeps finished one and a half lengths in front of True North, with Spotted Line third and Bushido fourth. The winner ran the six furlongs in 1:10 and paid $4.60. Silent Screen, owned by Sonny Werblin, who formerly owned the New York Jets, broke last and finished sixth in the ten-horse field.

Attendance was 28,215 and mutuel play $2,684,103. Mrs. Vince Lombardi, widow of the former Green Bay Packer and Washington Redskin coach, who had died of cancer the previous September, presented a trophy to Ussery, the winning jockey, after the race.

About an hour before the start of the game, as the crowd started filing into the Orange Bowl, several friends of John Newcombe, a public relations executive for the Goodyear Tire and Rubber Co., climbed into the company's blimp. The blimp, carrying an NBC television camera, was to hover over the Orange Bowl for the entire game.

"I couldn't get tickets for all of them," Newcombe said, "but I told them there was room in the blimp."

Outside the Orange Bowl, some scalpers were selling fifteen-dollar tickets for as much as one hundred dollars. But the supply was greater than the demand.

"The scalpers took a beating today," said a Miami police sergeant. "They were selling them at face value a half hour before the kickoff."

More than anyone, Baltimore's Earl Morrall wanted to redeem himself.

THE OPENING MATCHUPS

DALLAS ON OFFENSE

No.	Player	Ht.	Wt.	Pos.
22	Bob Hayes	5-11	185	WR
88	Reggie Rucker	6-2	190	WR
84	Pettis Norman	6-3	220	TE
70	Rayfield Wright	6-6	255	RT
61	Blaine Nye	6-4	251	RG
51	Dave Manders	6-2	250	C
76	John Niland	6-3	245	LG
73	Ralph Neely	6-6	265	LT
14	Craig Morton	6-4	214	QB
33	Duane Thomas	6-1	220	RB
32	Walt Garrison	6-0	205	FB

BALTIMORE ON DEFENSE

No.	Player	Ht.	Wt.	Pos.
35	Jim Duncan	6-2	200	RCB
47	Charlie Stukes	6-3	212	LCB
20	Jerry Logan	6-1	190	SS
78	Bubba Smith	6-7	295	LE
74	Billy Ray Smith	6-4	250	LT
32	Mike Curtis	6-2	232	MLB
76	Fred Miller	6-3	250	RT
85	Roy Hilton	6-6	240	RE
21	Rick Volk	6-3	195	FS
56	Ray May	6-1	230	LLB
83	Ted Hendricks	6-7	215	RLB

BALTIMORE ON OFFENSE

No.	Player	Ht.	Wt.	Pos.
33	Ed Hinton	6-0	200	WR
87	Roy Jefferson	6-2	195	WR
88	John Mackey	6-2	224	TE
71	Dan Sullivan	6-3	250	RT
75	John Williams	6-3	256	RG
50	Bill Curry	6-2	235	C
62	Glenn Ressler	6-3	250	LG
72	Bob Vogel	6-5	250	LT
19	John Unitas	6-1	196	QB
36	Norm Bulaich	6-1	218	RB
34	Tom Nowatzke	6-3	230	RB

DALLAS ON DEFENSE

No.	Player	Ht.	Wt.	Pos.
20	Mel Renfro	6-0	190	RCB
26	Herb Adderley	6-1	200	LCB
34	Cornell Green	6-3	208	SS
63	Larry Cole	6-4	250	LE
75	Jethro Pugh	6-6	260	LT
55	Lee Roy Jordan	6-1	221	MLB
74	Bob Lilly	6-5	260	RT
66	George Andrie	6-6	250	RE
41	Charlie Waters	6-1	193	FS
52	Dave Edwards	6-1	225	LLB
54	Chuck Howley	6-2	225	RLB

Unlike New Orleans, the pregame ceremony was not a bust.

Although the pregame show did not have as many problems as the previous year in New Orleans, it was not perfect by any means. The Air Force sent four of its jets over to buzz the stadium during the playing of the national anthem. The jets arrived two minutes after it ended.

What took place in the sixty minutes of football that followed could hardly be compared, in precision and performance, to watching Eugene Ormandy conduct the Philadelphia Orchestra; it was more like watching Spike Jones scrubbing washboards and squeezing bicycle horns in Wheeling, West Virginia. Super Bowl V was a collage of baggy-pants slapstick, a Marx Brothers movie in spiked sneakers. Many fans reacted with horror; as if, in anticipation of the sumptuousness of caviar, they discovered that the can contained tuna. The describing of Super Bowl V is best done clinically with a morphine chaser.

Chronologically, this was Super Bowl V — with each blunder listed in the order of occurrence rather than importance:

FIRST QUARTER

- With seven minutes gone, John Unitas of Baltimore threw an interception to Chuck Howley, a Dallas linebacker, who dove for the ball, caught it, juggled it, then finally returned it to the Baltimore 46-yard line — where Unitas, of all people, was the only obstacle between him and the goal line.
- Unitas tackled Howley.
- The Cowboys, in three plays, immediately proceeded to lose twenty-three yards back to their own 31 and were forced to punt. Ron Widby's kick sailed over the head of Ron Gardin, the Baltimore safety, who, instead of going back for it, puzzlingly went to his left instead, like a centerfielder misjudging a fly ball, and fumbled it. Cliff Harris recovered for Dallas.
- Taking over on the Colts' 9-yard line, Craig Morton, the Cowboys' quarterback, tried two running plays that went nowhere, then overthrew Reggie Rucker in the end zone on third down, spoiling a chance for an easy touchdown. (At this point, Mike Clark of Dallas reversed the trend by kicking a field goal from the 14-yard line, giving Dallas a 3–0 lead.)
- Late in the period, Morton threw down the sideline to Bob Hayes, who somehow caught the ball while sandwiched between Charlie Stukes and Jerry Logan of the Colts. The play carried to the Colts' 12-yard line, and a roughing-the-passer penalty called against Baltimore moved the ball even closer. Morton, however, single-handedly managed to move the Cowboys in the wrong direction after that. He hesitated on a pass play until Billy Ray Smith, the Baltimore tackle, was on the verge of spilling him for a sizable loss. Then he threw the ball to the most convenient Cowboy in sight, Blaine Nye, who happened to be a guard — and an ineligible receiver.

174

Craig Morton gives to Duane Thomas, but Baltimore wasn't giving.

Dallas' Chuck Howley intercepts a John Unitas pass.

The penalty cost Dallas fifteen yards. Then Morton failed to see Duane Thomas standing all alone on the sideline with Ralph Neely waiting to block for him and not a Colt in sight.

SECOND QUARTER

• After Mike Clark kicked his second field goal, giving Dallas a 6–0 lead, the Colts got the ball back. But Unitas still could not penetrate the Cowboys' defense with his passes and threw two incompletions. On third down he threw one intended for Eddie Hinton that flew far over his head. Hinton jumped high into the air and touched the ball with his fingertips, deflecting it toward Mel Renfro, a Cowboy corner back. Renfro, too, got a fingertip on the ball, but could not pluck it from the air. The ball finally settled in the arms of John Mackey, the Colts' tight end, who took it all the way for a touchdown. The play, covering seventy-five yards, was one to test the credibility of any defensive back — if it could have been proven that Renfro did not touch the ball, the play would have been called back. Rules state that two offensive players cannot touch the ball as receivers unless there is a lateral involved. Naturally, Renfro said he did not touch it. The officials said he did. Naturally, the officials won. The Colts were awarded the touchdown, tying the score at 6–6.

• Onto the field came Jim O'Brien, the Colts' rookie kicker and Air Force Academy dropout, to attempt the extra point. Since only 25 of 797 conversions failed in the NFL during the season, one could regard the successful kicking of placements as a foregone conclusion. But, Mark Washington of the Cowboys cleanly blocked O'Brien's kick, leaving the score at 6–6. "He came in from the left," said Earl Morrall, who was holding the ball for O'Brien. "O'Brien may have been a hair slow in kicking it, but the block was a good one, right off the chest." Tom Nowatzke didn't help matters for the Colts when he completely missed his block on Washington.

• Unitas, getting the ball back after a Dallas punt, continued to find the Cowboys' defense puzzling. Trying to elude a rush and finding no receivers open, he elected to run the ball — and fumbled it when hit by linebacker Lee Roy Jordan. Dallas, naturally, recovered on the Baltimore 28-yard line.

(At this point, the Cowboys put together their best offensive series of the day. Craig Morton hit Dan Reeves with a flare pass and Reeves ran it seventeen yards to the Colts' 11. After a short running gain, Morton threw a pass to Duane Thomas, who went the last seven yards for a touchdown. Mike Clark converted and Dallas went ahead by 13–6.)

• On the next series, Unitas, dropping back to pass, was leveled by George Andrie and the ball squirted into the hands of Renfro for still another interception. Unitas got up slowly and left the field, clutching his side. He suffered what was to be diagnosed later as a badly bruised rib cage.

John Mackey scores on a controversial play.

The Cowboy defense harasses Earl Morrall.

Rookie Norm Bulaich gallops through the Cowboys.

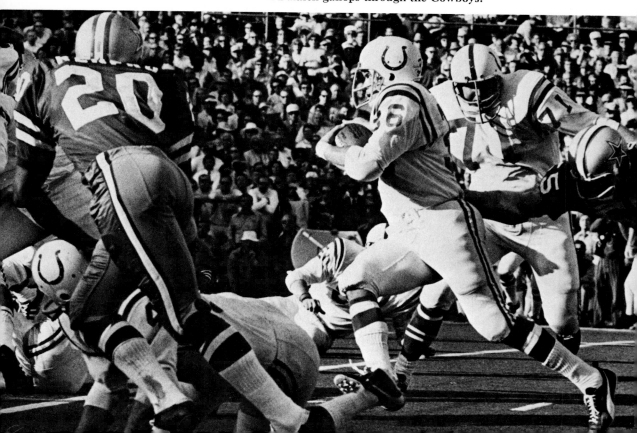

Into the game came Earl Morrall, the scapegoat for the 1969 loss to the Jets, and thoughts of Morrall vindicating Morrall for past blunders came into the heads of the 80,577 in attendance and countless millions watching on television sets in quiet living rooms. The first two times he handled the ball, Morrall looked as if he were taking on the Cowboys, the rest of the National League and Joe Namath's ghost all at the same time. He threw a perfect pass to Eddie Hinton for twenty-six yards, then hit Roy Jefferson on a similar pattern for twenty-one more on the very next play. Suddenly, Earl Morrall had put the Colts on the Dallas 2-yard line. But the next three plays brought him back down to AstroTurf and, no doubt, re-instilled visions of Al Atkinson and Johnny Sample into his crew-cut head. He sent Norm Bulaich, the rookie running back, into the line three straight times from the 2-yard line. But Bulaich failed to gain so much as an inch. With twenty-one seconds to go in the first half, with fourth and goal, the ball remained on the Cowboys' 2-yard line. Morrall called a time-out and went to the sideline to talk with Don McCafferty, his coach.

• McCafferty told him to go for the touchdown. The play would be a pass to Tom Mitchell in a corner of the end zone. Morrall went back in, called it, threw it and it bounced incomplete. Time ran out and the Cowboys led at the half 13–6.

The half-time show featured the singing of Anita Bryant, who did the "Battle Hymn of the Republic" as if it were 1866 again, so deep and spirited was her rendition. While the Southeast Missouri State College band marched along the AstroTurf, the crowd in the Orange Bowl critiqued the first half as the sloppiest on record in Super Bowl play. But if any anticipated both teams coming out in the second half with their heads straightened out, inspired and playing a high-caliber brand of football, their hopes were abruptly punctured.

THIRD QUARTER

• Jim Duncan of the Colts fumbled the opening kickoff and Richmond Flowers of the Cowboys recovered on the Baltimore 31.

• A few minutes later, Duncan vindicated himself. Dallas drove to the Baltimore 1-yard line, where Duane Thomas fumbled the ball. Duncan fell on it. "Thomas was trying to lunge over the goal line for the touchdown, with his hands stretched out to get the ball over the line," said Duncan. "He fell with his hands outstretched and I fell over his arms. The ball popped out and under me. I thought, 'This is my big chance.' I made sure I got the ball. I owed one for fumbling the kickoff."

• Later in the third period, with the score still 13–6, Dallas, the Colts tried a field goal. O'Brien kicked it, but it was far short. Mel Renfro, deep, instead of returning the kick, let it bounce — hoping it would go into the end zone for a touchback, giving Dallas possession on its own 20. Instead, the ball rolled dead on the Dallas 6-inch line.

FOURTH QUARTER

• On the first play of the last period, Earl Morrall, rushed hard by the Cowboys' George Andrie, threw a bad pass and Chuck Howley made his second interception of the day for Dallas. It was the sixth Baltimore turnover of the game, which, by now, had become genuinely interesting because of its lack of predictability. There were no somber Packer sweeps or precision Namath-to-Maynard passes in this one; Super Bowl V was one for the sandlots of Altoona, Pennsylvania.

• With nine minutes left and Dallas still leading, 13–6, Morrall resurrected the play that had made him look so bad two years earlier — the flea-flicker. He lateraled the ball to Sam Havrilak, a halfback who was once a quarterback at Bucknell. Havrilak was supposed to lateral back to Morrall, but when he looked for Morrall he did not see him; Jethro Pugh, a Dallas tackle of some dimension, was blocking the view. So, like a seasoned quarterback, Havrilak looked downfield and threw a pass for John Mackey, who was open. Before the ball reached Mackey, however, Eddie Hinton stepped in front of him and caught it instead and headed for the uncluttered end zone. But Hinton and the ball did not make it there simultaneously.

"I could see the end zone in front of me," said Hinton. "I was trying to work my way there when, all of a sudden, someone knocked the ball out of my hands from behind. I tried to get to it but someone else tackled me and I couldn't reach it." Cornell Green had knocked the ball from Hinton's arms and Mel Renfro had tackled him.

• The ball, meantime, was bouncing over the goal line. Several Colt and Cowboy players took turns recovering and refumbling it until the ball finally trickled out of the end zone. It was a touchback, so Dallas took possession on its own 20-yard line. It was Baltimore's seventh turnover, and one could imagine Casey Stengel, sitting near his bank vault in Glendale, California, asking Edna, "Can't anybody here play this game?"

• Immediately, the Cowboys tried a little onedownsmanship. From his own 20, Morton threw a pass to Walt Garrison, but Jim Duncan of Baltimore tipped it and the ball fell into the arms of Rick Volk, the Colts' safety, for still another interception. "We were in a good zone defense for their pattern," said Volk. "We had their outside receivers covered. Garrison came out of their backfield and down the middle. Duncan anticipated it, and when I caught the ball I thought I'd go all the way." As it was, he went from the Dallas 33 to the 3.

(From the 3-yard line, Baltimore scored its first touchdown of the day.

Tom Nowatzke scores the Colts' second touchdown.

Baltimore's Eddie Hinton feints against Lee Roy Jordan.

Morrall sent Tom Nowatzke into the line twice — and he scored on the second try, making it 13–12, Dallas. O'Brien, who could hardly be described as an outstanding kicker on this day, came into the game and delivered the extra point, tying it at 13. Pete Rozelle sat in his special box, hoping it would stay that way until the end — forcing a sudden-death playoff, which, presumably, would go a long way toward emblazoning the memory of the day's dramatics upon the walls of the Football Hall of Fame in Canton, Ohio. But there were also those who were hoping that one team or the other would score to avoid the sudden-death and the prolonged agony.)

• With a little over six minutes left, Ron Widby punted for Dallas and Baltimore was left to start another series deep in its own territory — the 5-yard line. Morrall unveiled the three-yards-and-a-cloud-of-AstroTurf offense by handing off three straight times to his backs up the middle. But the Colts were forced to punt again and Dallas regained possession with just under two minutes left on the Baltimore 48 — which, if not definite field-goal range, was mighty close to it. One could almost sense the years of frustration inside Dallas football fans coming to the surface, ready to release, like underground volcanos.

• But Morton, still lacking assertiveness, and a Cowboy lineman, not lacking it, conspired to forestall the erupting. Morton got trapped for a loss and the lineman was whistled for holding. The Cowboys were pushed back to their own 27-yard line. Morton dropped back to pass again and threw to Dan Reeves coming out of the backfield. Reeves almost caught it. Colt linebacker Mike Curtis intercepted and returned the ball to the Cowboys' 28-yard line (and avoided stuffing it in Reeves' face — a practice he deplored when Johnny Sample of the Jets had done it to the Colts two years ago).

Now, with less than a minute remaining in the game, Morrall was going to get one last, exasperating chance to make himself a hero in the Super Bowl. The only way he could botch it now was by dropping the handoff from his center. Morrall sent Bulaich up the middle twice, and Bulaich picked up three yards to the Dallas 25. With nine seconds left, Morrall called a time-out, and when it expired he returned to the field accompanied by O'Brien, the young man the Colts call "Lassie" in deference to his long hair. The ball would be spotted on the Dallas 32-yard line, with Morrall holding and Bill Curry snapping it.

Curry snapped, Morrall spotted and O'Brien put his foot into the ball. It sailed straight and stayed inside the right goalpost by seven feet, his best kick of the afternoon. As the final four seconds ran out, with the scoreboard showing Baltimore 16, Dallas 13, Bob Lilly, a defensive tackle who had played in all of the other Dallas disappointments, took off his helmet and threw it forty feet straight into the air. Somebody in the press box said it was the best Dallas throw of the game.

182

Jim O'Brien makes the kick that counts.

In the Baltimore locker room, reporters clustered around O'Brien, assuring him of instant bronzing.

"I was figuring on sudden-death," O'Brien said. "I figured I'd get a chance in sudden-death sometime. When Curtis made the interception, I tried to get the blocked extra point out of my mind. When I went onto the field, the Dallas line was yelling at me, trying to distract me . . . a rookie . . . they always do that.

"Then, for a second I remembered our practices — how Billy Ray Smith would do the hollering to distract me, and I said to myself, 'This isn't nothing but Billy Ray Smith.' But I knew then that I was going to either win it or lose it for us. Some of the guys started talking to me, and Tom Mitchell came over and told me, 'Don't worry about anything, just kick it.' Then Morrall told me not to worry about the wind . . . just kick it straight. I kicked it well, it felt good going off my foot. I knew it was good.

"Funny thing, my mom called me and told me we couldn't lose. She's big on astrology and she figured it all out. I believe in astrology, too. I was born February 2, 1947. This is the age of Aquarius, isn't it? I'm an Aquarius."

In another cubicle, John Unitas was explaining his injury to newsmen.

"With my right arm up, my ribs were open," he said. "He got me with his helmet or his shoulder. I don't know which. They hurt, but they're not broken. They took X-rays right here to find that out immediately. I could have gone back if they needed me.

"I'm happy for Earl. He did a fine job. I did not mind not going back in the game. That was the coach's decision. Earl was down in the dumps after our other Super Bowl, and it was great that he could come back."

McCafferty, after receiving a game ball from his players, said, "I knew Unitas was available, but I stuck with Earl because Earl was doing a fine job and I saw no reason to change."

In yet another corner of the dressing room, Billy Ray Smith and Jimmy Orr, two of the Colts' oldest players, were announcing their retirements from the game.

"It's all over now," said Billy Ray, thirty-six years old. "I just won fifteen thousand dollars. And see this blood on my pants? You ask me whose blood this is? My blood. This is my last game. What can I possibly do after this, come back here and have the coaches run me out?"

Orr, who did not play, said, "Billy Ray and I started together for the Rams. Then we were traded to the Steelers, and then he was traded to the Colts. He told the Colts to trade for me, so he's the one who got me here. Now we're going out together, just like we came in."

Billy Ray Smith: "What can I possibly do after this?"

In the Cowboys' locker room, Tom Landry was holding court, however disconsolately.

"We beat ourselves," he said. "The fumble by Duane Thomas and the two interceptions killed us. If Thomas scores, they have a lot of catching up to do. We would have been in firm control."

Newsmen, searching for Thomas for a comment or two, could not find him in the locker room. They were told he had dressed and left the stadium.

So, Super Bowl V, although far from an artistic success, did have a peculiar appeal — the end vindicated the means, as if O'Brien's kick had eradicated all the absurdities of the first fifty-nine minutes and fifty-one seconds, dwarfing them at the finish. The Colts re-embraced the egos they had left behind in the Orange Bowl two years earlier, and the Cowboys, as usual, snatched defeat from the jaws of victory.

But, to football connoisseurs, it set Super Bowling back . . . well, five years to be exact.

Wrote Red Smith in his syndicated column:

Space does not permit a catalogue of the crimes and misdemeanors, the mortal and venial sins, the errors of commission and omission that made up this exercise in foolishness. This is fortunate, for in spite of the Supreme Court's several tolerant rulings regarding what constitutes suitable reading for the young, some limits ought to be observed in a paper like this.

Wrote Tex Maule in Sports Illustrated:

Perhaps the game should be called the Blunder Bowl from now on. The Baltimore Colts are the new world champions but they won their first Super Bowl by default, not design. Prior to this ultimate flicker of excellence, the Colts had entertained 80,000 Miami fans and a television audience from the far reaches of West Germany to Japan with five fumbles, four of them recovered by Dallas, three interceptions and a blocked extra point. That ought to be enough to present any opponent with a ballgame, but Dallas is just not any opponent. Indeed, the Cowboys finally demonstrated that they had an even greater talent for making the boo-boo. And to think that television was worried that situation comedy was dead.

NEW YORK, Jan. 21 (AP) — The 1971 Super Bowl football game between the Baltimore Colts and the Dallas Cowboys on Jan. 17 attracted the largest television audience ever to watch a single sports event. According to the National Broadcasting Company, the game was seen in 31,670,000 homes by an audience of 64 million people.

SUPER BOWL
RECORDS

SUPER BOWL I

Kansas City Chiefs (AFL) .... 0 10 0 0 — 10
Green Bay Packers (NFL) .... 7 7 14 7 — 35

GB — McGee, pass from Starr 37 (Chandler kick)
KC — McClinton, pass from Dawson 7 (Mercer kick)
GB — Taylor, run 14 (Chandler kick)
KC — Mercer (FG) 31
GB — Pitts, run 5 (Chandler kick)
GB — McGee, pass from Starr 13 (Chandler kick)
GB — Pitts, run 1 (Chandler kick)

TEAM STATISTICS

	KANSAS CITY	GREEN BAY
Total First Downs	17	21
First Downs Rushing	4	10
First Downs Passing	12	11
First Downs by Penalty	1	0
Total Offensive Yardage	239	358
Total No. Offensive Plays	64	64
Net Rushing Yardage	72	130
Net Passing Yardage	167	228
Times Thrown and Yardage Lost Attempting to Pass	6-61	3-22
Passes Attempted-Completed-Had Intercepted	32-17-1	24-16-1
Punts — Number and Average	7-45.3	4-43.3
Fumbles — Number and Lost	1-0	1-0
Penalties — Number and Yards	4-26	4-40
No. and Yards Punt Returns	3-19	4-23
No. and Yards Interception Returns	1-0	1-50

INDIVIDUAL STATISTICS

RUSHING

KANSAS CITY

	Atts.	Yds.	LG	TD
Dawson	3	24	15	0
Garrett	6	17	9	0
McClinton	6	16	6	0
Beathard	1	14	14	0
Coan	3	1	3	0

GREEN BAY

	Atts.	Yds.	LG	TD
Taylor, J.	16	53	14	1
Pitts	11	45	12	2
Anderson, D.	4	30	13	0
Grabowski	2	2	2	0

PASSING

	Atts.	Comp.	Yds.	Int.	TD
Dawson	27	16	211	1	1
Beathard	5	1	17	0	0

	Atts.	Comp.	Yds.	Int.	TD
Starr	23	16	250	1	2
Bratkowski	1	0	0	0	0

RECEIVING

	No.	Yds.	TD
Burford	4	67	0
Taylor, O.	4	57	0
Garrett	3	28	0
McClinton	2	34	1
Arbanas	2	30	0
Carolan	1	7	0
Coan	1	5	0

	No.	Yds.	TD
McGee	7	138	2
Dale	4	59	0
Pitts	2	32	0
Fleming	2	22	0
Taylor, J.	1	−1	0

SUPER BOWL II

Green Bay Packers (NFL) .... 3 13 10 7 — 33
Oakland Raiders (AFL) 0   7   0 7 — 14

GB — Chandler (FG) 39
GB — Chandler (FG) 20
GB — Dowler, pass from Starr 62 (Chandler kick)
Oak — Miller, pass from Lamonica 23 (Blanda kick)
GB — Chandler (FG) 43
GB — Anderson, run 2 (Chandler kick)
GB — Chandler (FG) 31
GB — Adderley, pass interception 60 (Chandler kick)
Oak — Miller, pass from Lamonica 23 (Blanda kick)

TEAM STATISTICS

	GREEN BAY	OAKLAND
Total First Downs	19	16
First Downs Rushing	11	5
First Downs Passing	7	10
First Downs by Penalty	1	1
Total Offensive Yardage	322	293
Total No. Offensive Plays	69	57
Net Rushing Yardage	160	107
Net Passing Yardage	162	186
Times Thrown and Yardage Lost Attempting to Pass	4-40	3-22
Passes Attempted-Completed-Had Intercepted	24-13-0	34-15-1
Punts — Number and Average	6-39.0	6-44.0
Fumbles — Number and Lost	0-0	3-2
Penalties — Number and Yards	1-12	4-31
No. and Yards Punt Returns	5-35	5-12
No. and Yards Interception Returns	1-60	0-0

INDIVIDUAL STATISTICS
RUSHING

GREEN BAY	Atts.	Yds.	LG	TD	OAKLAND	Atts.	Yds.	LG	TD
Wilson	17	62	13	0	Dixon	12	54	14	0
Anderson	14	48	8	1	Todd	2	37	32	0
Williams	8	36	18	0	Banaszak	6	16	5	0
Starr	1	14	14	0					
Mercein	1	0	0	0					

PASSING

	Atts.	Comp.	Yds.	Int.	TD		Atts.	Comp.	Yds.	Int.	TD
Starr	24	13	202	0	1	Lamonica	34	15	208	1	2

RECEIVING

	No.	Yds.	TD		No.	Yds.	TD
Dale	4	43	0	Miller	5	84	2
Fleming	4	35	0	Banaszak	4	69	0
Anderson	2	18	0	Biletnikoff	2	10	0
Dowler	2	71	1	Cannon	2	25	0
McGee	1	35	0	Dixon	1	3	0
				Wells	1	17	0

SUPER BOWL III

New York Jets (AFL) . . . . 0 7 6 3 — 16
Baltimore Colts (NFL) . . . . 0 0 0 7 — 7

NY — Snell, run 4 (Turner kick)
NY — Turner (FG) 32
NY — Turner (FG) 30
NY — Turner (FG) 9
Balt — Hill, run 1 (Michaels kick)

TEAM STATISTICS

	NEW YORK	BALTIMORE
Total First Downs	21	18
First Downs Rushing	10	7
First Downs Passing	10	9
First Downs by Penalty	1	2
Total Offensive Yardage	337	324
Total No. Offensive Plays	74	64
Net Rushing Yardage	142	143
Net Passing Yardage	195	181
Times Thrown and Yardage Lost Attempting to Pass	2-11	0-0
Passes Attempted-Completed-Had Intercepted	29-17-0	41-17-4
Punts — Number and Average	4-38.8	3-44.3
Fumbles — Number and Lost	1-1	1-1
Penalties — Number and Yards	5-28	3-23
No. and Yards Punt Returns	1-0	4-34
No. and Yards Interception Returns	4-9	0-0

INDIVIDUAL STATISTICS

RUSHING

NEW YORK	Atts.	Yds.	LG	TD	BALTIMORE	Atts.	Yds.	LG	TD
Snell	30	121	12	1	Matte	11	116	58	0
Boozer	10	19	8	0	Hill	9	29	12	1
Mathis	3	2	1	0	Unitas	1	0	0	0
					Morrall	2	-2	0	0

PASSING

	Atts.	Comp.	Yds.	Int.	TD		Atts.	Comp.	Yds.	Int.	TD
Namath	28	17	206	0	0	Morrall	17	6	71	3	0
Parilli	1	0	0	0	0	Unitas	24	11	110	1	0

RECEIVING

	No.	Yds.	TD		No.	Yds.	TD
Sauer	8	133	0	Richardson	6	58	0
Snell	4	40	0	Orr	3	42	0
Mathis	3	20	0	Mackey	3	35	0
Lammons	2	13	0	Matte	2	30	0
				Hill	2	1	0
				Mitchell	1	15	0

SUPER BOWL IV

Minnesota Vikings (NFL) .... 0 0 7 0 — 7
Kansas City Chiefs (AFL) .... 3 13 7 0 — 23

KC — Stenerud (FG) 48
KC — Stenerud (FG) 32
KC — Stenerud (FG) 25
KC — Garrett, run 5 (Stenerud kick)
Minn — Osborn, run 5 (Cox kick)
KC — Taylor, pass from Dawson 46 (Stenerud kick)

TEAM STATISTICS

	MINNESOTA	KANSAS CITY
Total First Downs	13	18
First Downs Rushing	2	8
First Downs Passing	10	7
First Downs by Penalty	1	3
Total Offensive Yardage	239	273
Total No. Offensive Plays	50	62
(Incl. times thrown passing)		
Net Rushing Yardage	67	151
Total Rushing Plays	19	42
Net Passing Yardage	172	122
Times Thrown and Yardage Lost		
Attempting to Pass	3-27	3-20
Passes Attempted-Completed-Had Intercepted	28-17-3	17-12-1
Punts — Number and Average	3-37.0	4-48.5
Fumbles — Number and Lost	3-2	0-0
Penalties — Number and Yards	6-67	4-47
No. and Yards Punt Returns	2-18	1-0
No. and Yards Kickoff Returns	4-79	2-36
No. and Yards Interception Returns	1-0	3-24

INDIVIDUAL STATISTICS

RUSHING

MINNESOTA	Atts.	Yds.	LG	TD	KANSAS CITY	Atts.	Yds.	LG	TD
Brown	6	26	10	0	Garrett	11	39	6	1
Reed	4	17	15	0	Pitts	3	37	19	0
Osborn	7	15	4	1	Hayes	8	31	13	0
Kapp	2	9	7	0	McVea	12	26	9	0
					Dawson	3	11	11	0
					Holmes	5	7	7	0

PASSING

	Atts.	Comp.	Yds.	Int.	TD		Atts.	Comp.	Yds.	Int.	TD
Cuozzo	3	1	16	1	0	Dawson	17	12	142	1	1
Kapp	25	16	183	2	0						

RECEIVING

	No.	Yds.	TD		No.	Yds.	TD
Henderson	7	111	0	Taylor	6	81	1
Brown	3	11	0	Pitts	3	33	0
Beasley	2	41	0	Garrett	2	25	0
Reed	2	16	0	Hayes	1	3	0
Osborn	2	11	0				
Washington	1	9	0				

SUPER BOWL V

Baltimore Colts (AFC) 0   6   0   10 — 16
Dallas Cowboys (NFC) .... 3 10   0   0 — 13

Dal — Clark (FG) 14
Dal — Clark (FG) 30
Balt — Mackey, pass from Unitas 75 (kick failed)
Dal — Thomas, pass from Morton 7 (Clark kick)
Balt — Nowatzke, run 2 (O'Brien kick)
Balt — O'Brien (FG) 32

TEAM STATISTICS

	BALTIMORE	DALLAS
Total First Downs	14	10
First Downs Rushing	4	4
First Downs Passing	6	5
First Downs by Penalty	4	1
Total Offensive Yardage	329	215
Total No. Offensive Plays	56	59
(Incl. times thrown passing)		
Net Rushing Yardage	69	102
Total Rushing Plays	31	31
Net Passing Yardage	260	113
Times Thrown and Yardage Lost		
Attempting to Pass	0-0	2-14
Passes Attempted-Completed-Had Intercepted	25-11-3	26-12-3
Punts — Number and Average	4-41.5	9-41.7
Fumbles — Number and Lost	5-4	1-1
Penalties — Number and Yards	4-31	10-133
No. and Yards Punt Returns	5-12	3-9
No. and Yards Kickoff Returns	4-90	3-34
No. and Yards Interception Returns	3-57	3-22

INDIVIDUAL STATISTICS

RUSHING

BALTIMORE	Atts.	Yds.	LG	TD	DALLAS	Atts.	Yds.	LG	TD
Bulaich	18	28	8	0	Garrison	12	65	19	0
Nowatzke	10	33	0	1	Thomas	18	35	7	0
Unitas	1	4	4	0	Morton	1	2	2	0
Havrilak	1	3	3	0					
Morrall	1	1	1	0					

PASSING

	Atts.	Comp.	Yds.	TD	LG	Int.		Atts.	Comp.	Yds.	TD	LG	Int.
Unitas	9	3	88	1	75	2	Morton	26	12	127	1	41	3
Morrall	15	7	147	1	45	1							
Havrilak	1	1	25	0	25	0							

RECEIVING

	No.	Yds.	TD		No.	Yds.	TD
Mackey	2	80	1	Reeves	5	46	0
Jefferson	3	52	0	Thomas	4	21	1
Hinton	2	51	0	Garrison	2	19	0
Havrilak	2	27	0	Hayes	1	41	0
Bulaich	1	5	0				
Nowatzke	1	45	0				

ALL-TIME SUPER BOWL RECORDS

(Compiled by Elias Sports Bureau, courtesy of the NFL)

INDIVIDUAL RECORDS

SCORING

Most Points, Game
15 Don Chandler, G.B. 1968 (3-pat, 4-fg)

Most Touchdowns, Game
2 Max McGee, G.B. 1967 (2-p)
Elijah Pitts, G.B. 1967 (2-r)
Bill Miller, Oak. 1968 (2-p)

Most Points After Touchdown, Game
5 Don Chandler, G.B. 1967 (5-att)

Most Field Goals Attempted, Game
5 Jim Turner, N.Y. 1969

Most Field Goals, Game
4 Don Chandler, G.B. 1968

Longest Field Goal
48 Jan Stenerud, K.C. 1970

RUSHING

Most Attempts, Game
30 Matt Snell, N.Y. 1969

Most Yards Gained, Game
121 Matt Snell, N.Y. 1969

Longest Gain
58 Tom Matte, Balt. 1969

Most Touchdowns, Game
2 Elijah Pitts, G.B. 1967

PASSING

Most Attempts, Game
34 Daryle Lamonica, Oak. 1968
(15-comp)

Most Completions, Game
17 Joe Namath, N.Y. 1969 (28-att)

Highest Efficiency, Game
70.6 Len Dawson, K.C. 1970 (17-12)

Most Yards Gained, Game
250 Bart Starr, G.B. 1967

Longest Completion
75 John Unitas (to Mackey), Balt. 1971 (TD)

Most Touchdowns, Game
2 Bart Starr, G.B. 1967
Daryle Lamonica, Oak. 1968

Fewest Had Intercepted, Most Attempts, Game
0 Joe Namath, N.Y. 1969 (28-att)

PASS RECEPTIONS

Most Receptions, Game
8 George Sauer, N.Y. 1969 (133 yds)

Most Yards Gained, Game
138 Max McGee, G.B. 1967 (7 rec)

Longest Reception
75 John Mackey (from Unitas), Balt. 1971 (TD)

Most Touchdowns, Game
2 Max McGee, G.B. 1967
Bill Miller, Oak. 1968

INTERCEPTIONS BY

Most Interceptions By, Game
2 Randy Beverly, N.Y. 1969
Chuck Howley, Dallas 1971

Most Yards Gained, Game
60 Herb Adderley, G.B. 1968 (1)

Longest Gain
60 Herb Adderley, G.B. 1968 (TD)

Most Touchdowns, Game
1 Herb Adderley, G.B. 1968

PUNTING

Most Punts, Game
9 Ron Widby, Dallas 1971

Longest Punt
61 Jerrel Wilson, K.C. 1967

Highest Punting Average, Game (3 Min.)
48.5 Jerrel Wilson, K.C. 1970 (4)

PUNT RETURNS

Most Punt Returns, Game
5 Willie Wood, G.B. 1968 (35 yds)

Most Fair Catches, Game
3 Ron Gardin, Balt. 1971

Most Yards Gained, Game
35 Willie Wood, G.B. 1968 (5)

Longest Punt Return
31 Willie Wood, G.B. 1968

Highest Average, Game (3 Min.)
8.5 Tim Brown, Balt. 1969 (4)

Most Touchdowns, Game
None

KICKOFF RETURNS

Most Kickoff Returns, Game
4 Jim Duncan, Balt. 1971 (90 yds)
Bert Coan, K.C. 1967 (87 yds)

Most Yards Gained, Game
90 Jim Duncan, Balt. 1971 (4)

Longest Kickoff Return
33 Preston Pearson, Balt. 1969
Clint Jones, Minn. 1970

Highest Average, Game (3 Min.)
22.5 Jim Duncan, Balt. 1971

Most Touchdowns, Game
None

TEAM RECORDS

SCORING

Most Points, Game
35 Green Bay 1967

Fewest Points, Game
7 Baltimore 1969
  Minnesota 1970

Most Points, Both Teams, Game
47 Green Bay (33) vs. Oak. (14) 1968

Fewest Points, Both Teams, Game
23 Baltimore (7) vs. N.Y. (16) 1969

Most Points, Each Quarter
1st: 7 Green Bay 1967
2nd: 13 Green Bay 1968
         Kansas City 1970
3rd: 14 Green Bay 1967
4th: 10 Baltimore 1971

Most Points, Both Teams, Each Quarter
1st: 7 Green Bay (7) vs. K.C. (0) 1967
2nd: 20 Green Bay (13) vs. Oak. (7) 1968
3rd: 14 Green Bay (14) vs. K.C. (0) 1967
         Minnesota (7) vs. K.C. (7) 1970
4th: 14 Green Bay (7) vs. Oak. (7) 1968

Most Touchdowns, Game
5 Green Bay 1967

Fewest Touchdowns, Game
1 Kansas City 1967
  Baltimore 1969
  New York 1969
  Minnesota 1970
  Dallas 1971

Most Touchdowns, Both Teams, Game
6 Green Bay (5) vs. K.C. (1) 1967

Fewest Touchdowns, Both Teams, Game
2 Baltimore (1) vs. N.Y. (1) 1969

Most Points After Touchdown, Game
5 Green Bay 1967

Most Points After Touchdown, Both Teams, Game
6 Green Bay (5) vs. K.C. (1) 1967

Most Field Goals Attempted, Game
5 New York 1969

Most Field Goals Attempted, Both Teams, Game
7 New York (5) vs. Balt. (2) 1969

Most Field Goals, Game
4 Green Bay 1968

Most Field Goals, Both Teams, Game
4 Green Bay (4) vs. Oak. (0) 1968

FIRST DOWNS

Most First Downs, Game
21 Green Bay 1967
   New York 1969

Most First Downs, Both Teams, Game
39 New York (21) vs. Balt. (18) 1969

Most First Downs, Rushing, Game
11 Green Bay 1968

Most First Downs, Rushing, Both Teams, Game
17 New York (10) vs. Balt. (7) 1969

Most First Downs, Passing, Game
12 Kansas City 1967

Most First Downs, Passing, Both Teams, Game
23 Kansas City (12) vs. G.B. (11) 1967

Most First Downs, Penalty, Game
4 Baltimore 1971

NET YARDS GAINED
(Rushes & Passes)

Most Yards Gained, Game
358 Green Bay 1967

Most Yards Gained, Both Teams, Game
661 New York (337) vs. Balt. (324) 1969

RUSHING

Most Attempts, Game
43 New York 1969

Fewest Attempts, Game
19 Kansas City 1967
   Minnesota 1970

Most Attempts, Both Teams, Game
66 New York (43) vs. Balt. (23) 1969

Fewest Attempts, Both Teams, Game
52 Kansas City (19) vs. G.B. (33) 1967

Most Yards Gained, Game
160 Green Bay 1968

Fewest Yards Gained, Game
67 Minnesota 1970

Most Yards Gained, Both Teams, Game
285 Baltimore (143) vs. N.Y. (142) 1969

Fewest Yards Gained, Both Teams, Game
171 Baltimore (69) vs. Dallas (102) 1971

Most Touchdowns, Game
3 Green Bay 1967

Fewest Touchdowns, Game
0 Kansas City 1967
  Oakland 1968
  Dallas 1971

Most Touchdowns, Both Teams, Game
3 Green Bay (3) vs. K.C. (0) 1967

Fewest Touchdowns, Both Teams, Game
1 Oakland (0) vs. G.B. (1) 1968
  Baltimore (1) vs. Dallas (0) 1971

PASSING

Most Passes Attempted, Game
41 Baltimore 1969

Fewest Passes Attempted, Game
17 Kansas City 1970

Most Passes Attempted, Both Teams, Game
70 Baltimore (41) vs. N.Y. (29) 1969

Fewest Passes Attempted, Both Teams, Game
45   Kansas City (17) vs. Minn. (28) 1970

Most Passes Completed, Game
17   Kansas City 1967
     Baltimore 1969
     New York 1969
     Minnesota 1970

Fewest Passes Completed, Game
11   Baltimore 1971

Most Passes Completed, Both Teams, Game
34   Baltimore (17) vs. N.Y. (17) 1969

Fewest Passes Completed, Both Teams, Game
23   Baltimore (11) vs. Dallas (12) 1971

Most Yards Gained, Game
260   Baltimore 1971

Fewest Yards Gained, Game
122   Kansas City 1970

Most Yards Gained, Both Teams, Game
395   Green Bay (228) vs. K.C. (167) 1967

Fewest Yards Gained, Both Teams, Game
294   Kansas City (122) vs. Minn. (172) 1970

Most Times Tackled Attempting Passes, Game
6   Kansas City 1967

Fewest Times Tackled Attempting Passes, Game
0   Baltimore 1969
    Baltimore 1971

Most Times Tackled Attempting Passes, Both Teams, Game
9   Kansas City (6) vs. G.B. (3) 1967

Fewest Times Tackled Attempting Passes, Both Teams, Game
2   Baltimore (0) vs. N.Y. (2) 1969
    Baltimore (0) vs. Dallas (2) 1971

Most Touchdowns, Game
2   Green Bay 1967
    Oakland 1968

Fewest Touchdowns, Game
0   Baltimore 1969
    New York 1969
    Minnesota 1970

Most Touchdowns, Both Teams, Game
3   Green Bay (2) vs. K.C. (1) 1967
    Oakland (2) vs. G.B. (1) 1968

INTERCEPTIONS BY

Most Interceptions By, Game
4   New York 1969

Most Yards Gained, Game
60   Green Bay 1968

Most Interceptions By, Both Teams, Game
6   Baltimore (3) vs. Dallas (3) 1971

Most Touchdowns, Game
1   Green Bay 1968

PUNTING

Most Punts, Game
9   Dallas 1971

Fewest Punts, Game
3   Baltimore 1969
    Minnesota 1970

Most Punts, Both Teams, Game
13   Baltimore (4) vs. Dallas (9) 1971

Fewest Punts, Both Teams, Game
7   Baltimore (3) vs. N.Y. (4) 1969
    Minnesota (3) vs. K.C. (4) 1970

Highest Average, Game
48.5   Kansas City 1970 (4)

Lowest Average, Game
37.0   Minnesota 1970 (3)

PUNT RETURNS

Most Punt Returns, Game
5   Green Bay 1968
    Baltimore 1971

Fewest Punt Returns, Game
1   New York 1969
    Kansas City 1970

Most Punt Returns, Both Teams, Game
8   Green Bay (5) vs. Oak. (3) 1968
    Baltimore (5) vs. Dallas (3) 1971

Fewest Punt Returns, Both Teams, Game
3   Kansas City (1) vs. Minn. (2) 1970

Most Yards Gained, Game
35   Green Bay 1968

Fewest Yards Gained, Game
0   New York 1969 (1)
    Kansas City 1970 (1)

Most Yards Gained, Both Teams, Game
47   Green Bay (35) vs. Oak. (12) 1968

Fewest Yards Gained, Both Teams, Game
18   Kansas City (0) vs. Minn. (18) 1970

Highest Average Gain, Game
9.0   Minnesota 1970 (2)

KICKOFF RETURNS

Most Kickoff Returns, Game
7   Oakland 1968

Fewest Kickoff Returns, Game
1   New York 1969

Most Kickoff Returns, Both Teams, Game
10   Oakland (7) vs. G.B. (3) 1968

Fewest Kickoff Returns, Both Teams, Game
5   New York (1) vs. Balt. (4) 1969

Most Yards Gained, Game
130   Kansas City 1967

Fewest Yards Gained, Game
25   New York 1969 (1)

Most Yards Gained, Both Teams, Game
195   Kansas City (130) vs. G.B. (65) 1967

Fewest Yards Gained, Both Teams, Game
115   Kansas City (36) vs. Minn. (79) 1970

Highest Average Gain, Game
26.3   Baltimore 1969 (4)

ALL-TIME SUPER BOWL ROSTER

The following is a complete directory listing every player who has been on a Super Bowl roster in games I through V. Where a player did not play in the game, this is indicated by (dnp) following the Super Bowl numeral.

Name	Team	Game	Position	College
Abell, Bud	Kansas City	I	LB	Missouri
Adderley, Herb	G.B.-Dallas	I, II, V	DB	Michigan State
Alderman, Grady	Minnesota	IV	OT	Detroit
Aldridge, Lionel	Green Bay	I, II	DE	Utah State
Anderson, Bill	Green Bay	I	TE	Tennessee
Anderson, Donny	Green Bay	I, II	RB-P	Texas Tech
Andrie, George	Dallas	V	DE	Marquette
Arbanas, Fred	Kansas City	I, IV	TE	Michigan State
Archer, Dan	Oakland	II	OT	Oregon
Asher, Bob	Dallas	V	OT	Vanderbilt
Atkinson, Al	New York	III	LB	Villanova
Austin, Ocie	Baltimore	III	DB	Utah State
Baird, Bill	New York	III	DB	San Francisco State
Baker, Ralph	New York	III	LB	Penn State
Ball, Sam	Baltimore	III, V	OT	Kentucky
Banaszak, Pete	Oakland	II	RB	Miami (Fla.)
Beasley, John	Minnesota	IV	TE	California
Beathard, Pete	Kansas City	I	QB	Southern California
Bell, Bobby	Kansas City	I, IV	LB	Minnesota
Belser, Ceaser	Kansas City	IV	DB	Arkansas AM&N
Benson, Duane	Oakland	II	LB	Hamline
Beverly, Randy	New York	III	DB	Colorado State
Biggs, Verlon	New York	III	DE	Jackson State
Biletnikoff, Fred	Oakland	II	WR	Florida State
Biodrowski, Denny	Kansas City	I	G	Memphis State
Bird, Rodger	Oakland	II	DB	Kentucky
Birdwell, Dan	Oakland	II	DT	Houston
Blanda, George	Oakland	II	K	Kentucky
Boozer, Emerson	New York	III	RB	Maryland State
Bowman, Ken	Green Bay	I, II	C	Wisconsin
Boyd, Bob	Baltimore	III	DB	Oklahoma
Braase, Ordell	Baltimore	III	DE	South Dakota
Bratkowski, Zeke	Green Bay	I, II	QB	Georgia
Brown, Aaron	Kansas City	I, IV	DE	Minnesota
Brown, Bill	Minnesota	IV	RB	Illinois
Brown, Bob	Green Bay	I, II	DE	Arkansas AM&N
Brown, Tim	Baltimore	III	RB	Ball State
Brown, Tom	Green Bay	I, II	DB	Maryland
Brown, Willie	Oakland	II	DB	Grambling
Buchanan, Buck	Kansas City	I, IV	DT	Grambling

198

Name	Team	Game	Position	College
Budde, Ed	Kansas City	I, IV	G	Michigan State
Budness, Bill	Oakland	II	LB	Boston U.
Bulaich, Norm	Baltimore	V	RB	TCU
Burford, Chris	Kansas City	I	WR	Stanford
Caffey, Lee Roy	Green Bay	I, II	LB	Texas A&M
Cannon, Billy	Oakland	II	RB	LSU
Capp, Dick	Green Bay	II	TE-LB	Boston College
Carolan, Reg	Kansas City	I	TE	Idaho
Chandler, Don	Green Bay	I, II	K	Florida
Christy, Earl	New York	III	DB	Maryland State
Clark, Mike	Dallas	V	K	Texas A&M
Coan, Bert	Kansas City	I	RB	Kansas
Cole, Larry	Dallas	V	DE	Hawaii
Cole, Terry	Baltimore	III	RB	Indiana
Conners, Dan	Oakland	II	LB	Miami (Fla.)
Corey, Walt	Kansas City	I	LB	Miami (Fla.)
Cox, Fred	Minnesota	IV	K	Pittsburgh
Crane, Paul	New York	III	LB-C	Alabama
Crutcher, Tommy	Green Bay	I, II	LB	TCU
Culp, Curley	Kansas City	IV	DT	Arizona State
Cuozzo, Gary	Minnesota	IV	QB	Virginia
Curry, Bill	G.B.-Baltimore	I, III, V	C-LB	Georgia Tech
Curtis, Mike	Baltimore	III, V	LB	Duke
Dale, Carroll	Green Bay	I, II	WR	Virginia Tech
D'Amato, Mike	New York	III	DB	Hofstra
Daney, George	Kansas City	IV	G	Texas-El Paso
Davidson, Ben	Oakland	II	DE	Washington
Davis, Doug	Minnesota	IV (dnp)	T	Kentucky
Davis, Willie	Green Bay	I, II	DE	Grambling
Dawson, Len	Kansas City	I, IV	QB	Purdue
DeMidio, Tony	Kansas City	I	OT	West Chester St.
Dickson, Paul	Minnesota	IV	DT	Baylor
Ditka, Mike	Dallas	V	TE	Pittsburgh
Dixon, Hewritt	Oakland	II	RB	Florida A&M
Dockery, John	New York	III	DB	Harvard
Dowler, Boyd	Green Bay	I, II	WR	Colorado
Duncan, Jim	Baltimore	V	DB	Maryland State
East, Ron	Dallas	V	DT	Montana State
Edwards, Dave	Dallas	V	LB	Auburn
Eischeid, Mike	Oakland	II	P	Upper Iowa
Eller, Carl	Minnesota	IV	DE	Minnesota
Elliott, John	New York	III	DT	Texas
Flanigan, Jim	Green Bay	II	LB	Pittsburgh
Fleming, Marv	Green Bay	I, II	TE	Utah
Flores, Tom	Kansas City	IV (dnp)	QB	Pacific
Flowers, Richmond	Dallas	V	WR	Tennessee
Frazier, Wayne	Kansas City	I	C	Auburn
Gardin, Ron	Baltimore	V	DB	Arizona

Name	Team	Game	Position	College
Garrett, Mike	Kansas City	I, IV	RB	Southern California
Garrison, Walt	Dallas	V	RB	Oklahoma State
Gaubatz, Dennis	Baltimore	III	LB	LSU
Gilliam, Jon	Kansas City	I	C	East Texas State
Gillingham, Gale	Green Bay	I, II	G	Minnesota
Goode, Tom	Baltimore	V	C	Mississippi St.
Gordon, Cornell	New York	III	DB	N. Carolina A&T
Grabowski, Jim	Green Bay	I, II (dnp)	RB	Illinois
Grant, Bob	Baltimore	V	LB	Wake Forest
Grantham, Larry	New York	III	LB	Mississippi
Grayson, Dave	Oakland	II	DB	Oregon
Green, Cornell	Dallas	V	DB	Utah State
Gregg, Forrest	Green Bay	I, II	T	SMU
Grim, Bob	Minnesota	IV	WR	Oregon State
Hackbart, Dale	Minnesota	IV	DB	Wisconsin
Hagberg, Roger	Oakland	II	RB	Minnesota
Hargrove, Jim	Minnesota	IV	LB	Howard Payne
Harris, Bill	Minnesota	IV	RB	Colorado
Harris, Cliff	Dallas	V	DB	Ouachita U.
Hart, Doug	Green Bay	I, II	DB	Arlington State
Harvey, Jim	Oakland	II	G	Mississippi
Hathcock, Dave	Green Bay	I	DB	Memphis State
Havrilak, Sam	Baltimore	V	RB	Bucknell
Hawkins, Alex	Baltimore	III	WR	South Carolina
Hawkins, Wayne	Oakland	II	G	Pacific
Hayes, Bob	Dallas	V	WR	Florida A&M
Hayes, Wendell	Kansas City	IV	RB	Humboldt State
Headrick, Sherrill	Kansas City	I	LB	TCU
Henderson, John	Minnesota	IV	WR	Michigan
Hendricks, Ted	Baltimore	V	LB	Miami (Fla.)
Herman, Dave	New York	II	TE	Michigan State
Herock, Ken	Oakland	III	OT	West Virginia
Hilgenberg, Wally	Minnesota	IV	LB	Iowa
Hill, Calvin	Dallas	V	RB	Yale
Hill, Dave	Kansas City	I, IV	OT	Auburn
Hill, Jerry	Baltimore	III, V	RB	Wyoming
Hill, Winston	New York	III	OT	Texas Southern
Hilton, Roy	Baltimore	III, V	DE	Jackson State
Hinton, Ed	Baltimore	V	WR	Oklahoma
Holmes, Robert	Kansas City	IV	RB	Southern U.
Holub, E. J.	Kansas City	I, IV	LB-C	Texas Tech
Horn, Don	Green Bay	II (dnp)	QB	San Diego State
Hornung, Paul	Green Bay	I	RB	Notre Dame
Howley, Chuck	Dallas	V	LB	West Virginia
Hudson, Jim	New York	III	DB	Texas
Hunt, Bobby	Kansas City	I	DB	Auburn
Hurston, Chuck	Kansas City	I, IV	DE-LB	Auburn
Hyland, Bob	Green Bay	II	C	Boston College

Name	Team	Game	Position	College
Jefferson, Roy	Baltimore	V	WR	Utah
Jeter, Bob	Green Bay	I, II	DB	Iowa
Johnson, Cornelius	Baltimore	III, V	G	Virginia Union
Johnson, Curley	New York	III	P	Houston
Jones, Clint	Minnesota	IV	RB	Michigan
Jordan, Henry	Green Bay	I, II	DT	Virginia
Jordan, Lee Roy	Dallas	V	LB	Alabama
Kapp, Joe	Minnesota	IV	QB	California
Kassulke, Karl	Minnesota	IV	DB	Drake
Kearney, Jim	Kansas City	IV	DB	Prairie View
Keating, Tom	Oakland	II	DT	Michigan
Kiner, Steve	Dallas	V	LB	Tennessee
Kocourek, Dave	Oakland	II	TE	Wisconsin
Kostelnik, Ron	Green Bay	I, II	DT	Cincinnati
Kramer, Jerry	Green Bay	I, II	G	Idaho
Kramer, Kent	Minnesota	IV	TE	Minnesota
Krause, Paul	Minnesota	IV	DB	Iowa
Kruse, Bob	Oakland	II	G	Wayne State
Lammons, Pete	New York	III	TE	Texas
Lamonica, Daryle	Oakland	II	QB	Notre Dame
Lanier, Willie	Kansas City	IV	LB	Morgan State
Larsen, Gary	Minnesota	IV	DT	Concordia (Minn.)
Laskey, Bill	Oakland	II	LB	Michigan
Lassiter, Ike	Oakland	II	DE	St. Augustine
Lee, Bob	Minnesota	IV	QB-P	Pacific
Lee, David	Baltimore	III, V	P	Louisiana Tech
Lewis, D. D.	Dallas	V	LB	Mississippi State
Lilly, Bob	Dallas	V	DT	TCU
Lindsey, Jim	Minnesota	IV	RB	Arkansas
Liscio, Tony	Dallas	V (dnp)	OT	Tulsa
Livingston, Mike	Kansas City	IV	QB	SMU
Logan, Jerry	Baltimore	III, V	DB	West Texas State
Long, Bob	Green Bay	I, II	WR	Wichita
Lothamer, Ed	Kansas City	IV	DT	Michigan State
Lyles, Lenny	Baltimore	III	DB	Louisville
Lynch, Jim	Kansas City	IV	LB	Notre Dame
Mack, Red	Green Bay	I	WR	Notre Dame
Mackbee, Earsell	Minnesota	IV	DB	Utah State
Mackey, John	Baltimore	III, V	TE	Syracuse
Maitland, Jack	Baltimore	V	RB	Williams
Manders, Dave	Dallas	V	C	Michigan State
Marsalis, Jim	Kansas City	IV	DB	Tennessee State
Marshall, Jim	Minnesota	IV	DE	Ohio State
Mathis, Bill	New York	III	RB	Clemson
Matte, Tom	Baltimore	III	RB	Ohio State
Maxwell, Tom	Baltimore	V	DB	Texas A&M
May, Ray	Baltimore	V	LB	Southern California
Maynard, Don	New York	III	WR	Texas Western

Name	Team	Game	Position	College
Mays, Jerry	Kansas City	I, IV	DE	SMU
McAdams, Carl	New York	III	DT-LB	Oklahoma
McClinton, Curtis	Kansas City	I, IV	RB-TE	Kansas
McCloughan, Kent	Oakland	II	DB	Nebraska
McGee, Max	Green Bay	I, II	WR	Tulane
McGill, Mike	Minnesota	IV	LB	Notre Dame
McVea, Warren	Kansas City	IV	RB	Houston
Mercein, Chuck	Green Bay	II	RB	Yale
Mercer, Mike	Kansas City	I	K	Arizona State
Merz, Curt	Kansas City	I	G	Iowa
Michaels, Lou	Baltimore	III	DE-K	Kentucky
Miller, Bill	Oakland	II	WR	Miami (Fla.)
Miller, Fred	Baltimore	III, V	DT	LSU
Mitchell, Tom	Baltimore	III, V	TE	Bucknell
Mitchell, Willie	Kansas City	I, IV	DB	Tennessee State
Moorman, Mo	Kansas City	IV	G	Texas A&M
Morrall, Earl	Baltimore	III, V	QB	Michigan State
Morton, Craig	Dallas	V	QB	California
Namath, Joe	New York	III	QB	Alabama
Neely, Ralph	Dallas	V	G	Oklahoma
Neidert, John	New York	III	LB	Louisville
Newsome, Billy	Baltimore	V	DE	Grambling
Nichols, Robbie	Baltimore	V	LB	Tulsa
Niland, John	Dallas	V	G	Iowa
Nitschke, Ray	Green Bay	I, II	LB	Illinois
Norman, Pettis	Dallas	V	TE	Johnson C. Smith
Nowatzke, Tom	Baltimore	V	RB	Indiana
Nye, Blaine	Dallas	V	G	Stanford
Oates, Carleton	Oakland	II	DE	Florida A&M
O'Brien, Jim	Baltimore	V	K	Cincinnati
Orr, Jimmy	Baltimore	III, V (dnp)	WR	Georgia
Osborn, Dave	Minnesota	IV	RB	Notre Dame
Otto, Gus	Oakland	II	LB	Missouri
Otto, Jim	Oakland	II	C	Miami (Fla.)
Page, Alan	Minnesota	IV	DT	Notre Dame
Parilli, Babe	New York	III	QB	Kentucky
Pearson, Preston	Baltimore	III	RB	Illinois
Perkins, Ray	Baltimore	III, V	WR	Alabama
Philbin, Gerry	New York	III	DE	Buffalo
Pitts, Elijah	Green Bay	I	RB	Philander Smith
Pitts, Frank	Kansas City	I, IV	WR	Southern U.
Ply, Bobby	Kansas City	I	DB	Baylor
Podolak, Ed	Kansas City	IV	RB	Iowa
Porter, Ron	Baltimore	III	LB	Idaho
Powers, Warren	Oakland	II	DB	Nebraska
Prudhomme, Remi	Kansas City	IV	C	LSU
Pugh, Jethro	Dallas	V	DT	Elizabeth City St.
Rademacher, Bill	New York	III	WR	Northern Michigan

Name	Team	Game	Position	College
Rasmussen, Randy	New York	III	G	Kearney State
Reed, Oscar	Minnesota	IV	RB	Colorado State
Reeves, Dan	Dallas	V	RB	South Carolina
Reilly, Mike	Minnesota	IV (dnp)	LB	Iowa
Renfro, Mel	Dallas	V	DB	Oregon
Ressler, Glenn	Baltimore	III, V	G	Penn State
Reynolds, Al	Kansas City	I	G	Tarkio (Mo.)
Rice, Andy	Kansas City	I	DT	Texas Southern
Richards, Jim	New York	III	DB	Virginia Tech
Richardson, Gloster	Kansas City	IV	WR	Jackson State
Richardson, Jeff	New York	III	OT-C	Michigan State
Richardson, Willie	Baltimore	III	WR	Jackson State
Robinson, Dave	Green Bay	I, II	LB	Penn State
Robinson, Johnny	Kansas City	I, IV	DB	LSU
Rochester, Paul	New York	III	DT	Michigan State
Rowser, John	Green Bay	II	DB	Michigan
Rucker, Reggie	Dallas	V	WR	Boston U.
Sample, John	New York	III	DB	Maryland State
Sauer, George	New York	III	WR	Texas
Schmitt, John	New York	III	C	Hofstra
Schuh, Harry	Oakland	II	OT	Memphis State
Sellers, Goldie	Kansas City	IV	DB	Grambling
Sharockman, Ed	Minnesota	IV	DB	Pittsburgh
Sherman, Rod	Oakland	II (dnp)	WR	Southern California
Shinnick, Don	Baltimore	III	LB	UCLA
Skoronski, Bob	Green Bay	I, II	OT	Indiana
Sligh, Richard	Oakland	II	DT	North Carolina Coll.
Smith, Billy Ray	Baltimore	III, V	OT	Arkansas
Smith, Bubba	Baltimore	III, V	DE	Michigan State
Smith, Fletcher	Kansas City	I	DB	Tennessee A&I
Smith, Steve	Minnesota	IV	DE	Michigan
Smolinski, Mark	New York	III	RB	Wyoming
Snell, Matt	New York	III	RB	Ohio State
Starr, Bart	Green Bay	I, II	QB	Alabama
Staubach, Roger	Dallas	V (dnp)	QB	Navy
Stein, Bob	Kansas City	IV	LB	Minnesota
Stenerud, Jan	Kansas City	IV	K	Montana State
Stincic, Tom	Dallas	V	LB	Michigan
Stover, Smokey	Kansas City	I	LB	Northeast Louisiana
Stroud, Morris	Kansas City	IV	TE	Clark College
Stukes, Charles	Baltimore	III, V	DB	Maryland State
Sullivan, Dan	Baltimore	III, V	G	Boston College
Sunde, Milt	Minnesota	IV	G	Minnesota
Svihus, Bob	Oakland	II	OT	Southern California
Szymanski, Dick	Baltimore	III	C	Notre Dame
Talamini, Bob	New York	III	G	Kentucky
Taylor, Jim	Green Bay	I	RB	LSU
Taylor, Otis	Kansas City	I, IV	WR	Prairie View

Name	Team	Game	Position	College
Thomas, Duane	Dallas	V	RB	West Texas State
Thomas, Emmitt	Kansas City	I, IV	DB	Bishop College
Thomas, Gene	Kansas City	I	RB	Florida A&M
Thompson, Steve	New York	III	DE	Washington
Thurston, Fred	Green Bay	I, II	G	Valparaiso
Tingelhoff, Mick	Minnesota	IV	C	Nebraska
Todd, Larry	Oakland	II	RB	Arizona State
Toomay, Pat	Dallas	V	DE	Vanderbilt
Trosch, Gene	Kansas City	IV	DE	Miami (Fla.)
Turner, Bake	New York	III	WR	Texas Tech
Turner, Jim	New York	III	K	Utah State
Tyrer, Jim	Kansas City	I, IV	OT	Ohio State
Unitas, John	Baltimore	III, V	QB	Louisville
Upshaw, Gene	Oakland	II	G	Texas A&I
Vandersea, Phil	Green Bay	I	RB	Massachusetts
Vellone, Jim	Minnesota	IV	G	South Carolina
Vogel, Bob	Baltimore	III, V	OT	Ohio State
Volk, Rick	Baltimore	III, V	DB	Michigan
Walton, Sam	New York	III	OT	East Texas State
Ward, Jim	Baltimore	III (dnp)	QB	Gettysburg
Warwick, Lonnie	Minnesota	IV	LB	Tennessee Tech
Washington, Gene	Minnesota	IV	WR	Michigan State
Washington, Mark	Dallas	V	DB	Morgan State
Waters, Charlie	Dallas	V	DB	Clemson
Weatherwax, Jim	Green Bay	I, II	DE-DT	Los Angeles State
Welch, Claxton	Dallas	V	RB	Oregon
Wells, Warren	Oakland	II	WR	Texas Southern
West, Charlie	Minnesota	IV	DB	Texas-El Paso
White, Ed	Minnesota	IV	G	California
Widby, Ron	Dallas	V	P	Tennessee
Williams, Howie	Oakland	II	DB	Howard U.
Williams, John	Baltimore	III, V	G	Minnesota
Williams, Sidney	Baltimore	III	LB	Southern U.
Williams, Travis	Green Bay	II	RB	Arizona State
Williamson, Fred	Kansas City	I	DB	Northwestern
Williamson, John	Oakland	II	LB	Louisiana Tech
Wilson, Ben	Green Bay	II	RB	Southern California
Wilson, Jerrel	Kansas City	I, IV	P	Southern Mississippi
Winston, Roy	Minnesota	IV	LB	LSU
Wood, Willie	Green Bay	I, II	DB	Southern California
Wright, George	Baltimore	V (dnp)	DT	Sam Houston
Wright, Rayfield	Dallas	V	OT	Fort Valley State
Wright, Steve	Green Bay	I, II (dnp)	OT	Alabama
Yary, Ron	Minnesota	IV	OT	Southern California

INDEX

206